CHAMPIONS OF LABOR

CHAMPIONS
OF
LABOR

by David F. Selvin

Illustrated with photographs

ABELARD-SCHUMAN
London   New York   Toronto

BOOKS BY DAVID F. SELVIN

CHAMPIONS OF LABOR

SAM GOMPERS *Labor's Pioneer*

Library of Congress Catalogue Card Number 67-16836

Standard Book Number: 200.71723.5

LONDON	NEW YORK	TORONTO
Abelard-Schuman	*Abelard-Schuman*	*Abelard-Schuman*
Limited	*Limited*	*Canada Limited*
8 King St. WC2	*257 Park Ave. S.*	*200 Yorkland Blvd.*
	10010	*425*

An Intext Publisher

Printed in the United States of America

To the memory
of my mother and father

CONTENTS

PHOTOGRAPHS

A Very Brief Foreword

HERE ARE short sketches of the lives and work of thirteen leaders of American labor. Each in his own way played a significant role in the course and development of the American trade union movement. Each left an imprint on it; each left the movement different from the way he found it. All were driven by the swirling currents of their times; yet none can accurately be described as merely a pawn of large impersonal forces. Personality and the tides of the time play and counterplay endlessly in their lives, one often indistinguishable from the other.

These thirteen have been chosen partly because their contributions to the labor movement have been especially meaningful and partly because they are fascinating personalities in their own right. Taken together, they encompass in their lives well over a hundred years of the American trade union movement — its flood and ebb, its shifting goals and changing course, the forces and counterforces that shape and endlessly reshape it. This broad panorama of unionism has been my chief underlying concern, the thread that runs (even though erratically at times) the length of the warp.

Some of the sketches are incomplete — in some cases, because the subjects are still active and vigorous and the end of their stories is not yet written. In other cases it is because I felt that the balance of their careers was less relevant to the story I wanted to tell. Each has — or, I hope, will one day have — at least a book of his own. I have not attempted to do more than trace, with fairly broad strokes, the chronicles of the trade unions. I have consequently been compelled to shrink important episodes into manageable size and pass over countless people and places and events. These, too, need to be filled in to see the picture in all its light and shadow. I hope these sketches and their broad picture will serve as an encouragement.

Plainly, I owe an immeasurable debt to countless others — historians and economists, trade union leaders and members, as well as editors, politicians and philosophers — from whose works I have gleaned the essentials of the biographies in these pages. The list is long; I am compelled to acknowledge my debt with only this brief, impersonal word of thanks and appreciation. They are, at the same time, absolved of any responsibility; the judgments and the errors are my own.

DAVID F. SELVIN

12

CHAPTER ONE
The Beginning

".. . the good Lord deliver us"

ONE MORNING in March in the year 1806, in the mayor's court of the city of Philadelphia, eight men solemnly, expectantly faced a jury. They were journeyman shoemakers, these eight men, and members of the Society of Cordwainers. They were accused of conspiring to raise their wages.

With their fellow society members, they had agreed on a rate of pay for making shoes. They had agreed, too, they would never work for less or with anyone who did. "They would not work in the same shop," the society told one reluctant shoemaker, "nor board nor lodge in the same house, nor would they work at all for the same employer."

The prosecution claimed that the law of Pennsylvania made these actions a criminal conspiracy. Any combination intended to raise wages was a crime against worker and employer and, most of all, against the state. It interfered with the growth of manufacturing. It disrupted the "natural law" of supply and demand. Such combinations had been crimes under the common law of England and — the prosecution contended — England's common law was now the common law of Pennsylvania.

Nothing of the sort, the defense countered. The shoemakers were free Americans; they were entitled to join together to better their conditions No law compelled one man to work with another. Besides, the master cordwainers had their own society. They combined to set the prices of the shoes they sold. The scale of wages had long been settled between them and their journeymen. "Shall all others," it was asked, "except only the industrious mechanics be allowed to meet and plot; merchants to determine their prices current, or settle the markets, politicians to electioneer, sportsmen for horseracing and games, ladies and gentlemen for balls, parties and bouquets; and yet these poor men be indicted for combining against starvation?" England's common law had no bearing on the matter; it no longer applied. It could not survive the Declaration of Independence without curbing the natural and inalienable rights of men. So the defense argued.

Recorder Moses Levy, presiding over the trial, instructed the jury: "A combination of workmen to raise their wages may be considered in a twofold point of view: one of benefit to themselves . . . the other is to injure those who do not join the society. The rule of law condemns both." He warned the jury what would happen: workmen would be demoralized, trade in the city destroyed, "the pockets of the whole community [would be left] to the discretion of those concerned." "Never," erupted an editorial in the Philadelphia *Aurora,* "did we hear a charge to a jury delivered in a more prejudiced and partial manner. . . ."

The fate of the eight shoemakers was handed over to the jury, which returned the expected verdict: "We find the defendants guilty of a combination to raise their wages." Recorder Levy fined the men eight dollars each and court costs. Pleaded the *Aurora*: ". . . from such court recorders and juries, good lord deliver us."

The court's findings echoed across the young nation. In at least nineteen cases in five states, workers faced charges of criminal conspiracy solely for joining or supporting a labor union. Not until 1842 was the taint erased, and then only in part. In that year, a Massachusetts court ruled that a union could properly and lawfully seek to improve wages and working conditions; if it used lawful means to achieve its goals, it would not be a criminal conspiracy. The ruling eased the fear that merely joining a union would result in criminal charges. It opened the way for workers to organize. But it gave the courts almost unlimited power to decide what goals were proper, what means were lawful. That power to approve — or disapprove — a union's goals and methods became in the years ahead a sharp and vengeful weapon.

The dark shadow of criminal charges was only one factor that shaped the place of labor unions in the nation's early years. Another was the simple fact that most Americans earned their livelihood in agriculture — in 1820, for instance, more than eight out of every ten. Of the two in each ten who made their living in other occupations, many were skilled craftsmen: carpenters and cabinet makers, shoemakers, leather workers, blacksmiths, tailors, glaziers, weavers. From them came the first tentative, groping union movement.

The expanding local market drove them to organize. Here, for instance, was a shoemaker conducting a quiet, made-to-order business. With the local market for his shoes expanding, he found it convenient to store up some of the more common sizes — perhaps hiring a new apprentice boy or a journeyman to help him. Now his business shifted

from custom-made shoes to ready-made shoes; he became
something of a merchant-capitalist. He put up capital to
buy raw materials and pay his employees. Soon he stood
apart; instead of being a fellow journeyman, he was an
employer. The journeymen and apprentices he hired no
longer were independent craftsmen; they were employees,
dependent on wages.

So, soon after the revolution, in the latter years of the
eighteenth century, these new employees formed combinations or unions. They tried to protect their wage rates
and to control the entrance of new men into the trade.
The carpenters in Philadelphia went on strike in 1791,
the Philadelphia cordwainers formed a local union in
1792, and the New York printers in 1794. Sometimes they
demanded higher wages, sometimes they protested a reduction in pay. They organized to provide their members
with sickness or funeral benefits. In the process they
developed some of the techniques that became fixtures on
the union scene.

On occasion the mechanics simply adopted a scale of
wages and announced they would work for no less. The
employers were likely, though, to insist on talking it over.
In this way, an early and primitive form of collective
bargaining emerged. The union named a "tramping committee" to visit the shops and make sure its wages were
being observed. Later it paid one of its members to police
its understanding with the employers — this was the "walking delegate," later the "business agent."

The skilled journeymen wanted to maintain the level
of skill; they were reluctant to see their trade flooded
with new, half-trained mechanics or untrained boys. They
sought some control over the rules of apprenticeship. And,
at times, their employers also joined forces — sometimes to

16

deal with their already-united employees, sometimes to rid themselves of men who joined the union or of the union itself.

Recurring depressions toppled the unions like tenpins. Wave upon wave of immigration faced the union men with growing, low-wage competition for jobs. As the nation grew, constantly workers moved westward. Unions organized, struggled to survive, then faded away; others formed in their places. At times — and especially in the 1830s — workingmen turned to politics. They supported other political parties or they organized their own. They demanded — and won — the right to vote. They campaigned for public schools and free public education and won them, too. They fought against imprisonment for debt. But their political parties, like their unions, flared briefly, then died away.

Still another force in encouraging workingmen to organize unions was the Industrial Revolution — the rapid growth of factory work spurred by the spreading use of labor-saving machinery and power-driven tools. Factory production separated the worker from his tools; it made him dependent on the factory — and on wages — for his livelihood. Large factories concentrated working people in cities and towns near the available jobs. And, as the nineteenth century neared its halfway mark, local markets began to blend into one another. The national market began to emerge.

In the 1850s alone, railroad mileage climbed from 8,389 to nearly 31,000. In 1812, it took a hardy traveler six days by stagecoach to go from Pittsburgh to Philadelphia. In 1854, he could make the trip by rail in less than a day. Rail lines stretched westward to Chicago, Cincinnati, St. Louis, then across the continent. Stoves made in Albany,

New York, were displayed in St. Louis, Missouri, alongside stoves made in Detroit, Michigan. A local monopoly in one city was now forced to compete with other manufacturers hundreds of miles away. Products from anywhere east of the Mississippi competed for customers throughout the area; workers from anywhere in the area competed for the available jobs. "Our vast occupations," explained *Fincher's Trade Review*, a prominent labor paper of the day, "are influenced by the most distant sections of the country, and in some cases by our neighboring nations."

Hat finishers reorganized their union in the 1840s. Printers formed the National — later the International — Typographical Union in the early 1850s. Coal miners, iron workers, machinists and blacksmiths and molders were among the many trades that organized local unions. As local unions learned that they shared a common cause, they began to think in terms of national unions. The Machinists and Blacksmiths, for instance, organized in 1859. The men joined in a list of grievances against their employers' "unfair dealing." They charged that the employers were taking on "as many apprentices as could possibly be worked"; labor-saving machinery, they said, made it possible to get as much work from an apprentice as from a journeyman. They objected, too, to "the peremptory dismissal of workmen." In dull times, men with families to support would find themselves out of work, while the shops, whose doors were closed to them, were filled with apprentice boys.

CHAPTER TWO

William H. Sylvis

"I love the Union cause"

IN 1855, the molders in a foundry in Philadelphia organized a union. "In the present organization of society," they declared, "laborers single-handed are powerless . . . but combined there is no power of wrong that they may not openly defy." Two years later, a notice went up in the foundry that their pay would be cut 12 per cent. Faced with this "wrong," the union prepared its defiance. It called the men out on strike.

One of the molders was twenty-seven-year-old William H. Sylvis. Though he was not a member of the union, he walked out with the rest. He joined in a pledge that none of them would return to work at the reduced wages. Sylvis was made a member of the "Committee on Corners," whose job it was to picket the shop, so that "no strangers should be permitted to take the places of the strikers without first being warned of the reasons that had prompted them to cease work." After some weeks, though, some men went back to work. Sylvis was among those who kept their word and held out still a little longer. He was admitted to the union and a few weeks later — despite some doubt about his ability to write — was made secretary.

Sylvis was the second son of Nicholas Sylvis of Armagh, a town, it was recorded, "of most trifling size," not far from Pittsburgh, Pennsylvania. Nicholas was a carriage maker by trade, a master when business was good, a journeyman when work was hard to find. He had operated his own shop until the depression of 1837 wiped him out. He took to the roads in search of work.

Young William was placed with a Mr. Pawling, a well-to-do and educated farmer who became a member of the state legislature. William did the farm work and chores in return for his keep. Frequently on Sundays he visited with his family. In the winter months, Pawling taught him "his letters and to spell a little." He gave him access to his library, and the boy made good use of it — a habit that was to stay with him during his relatively short life.

When he was seventeen, William returned to his family and went to work in his father's carriage shop. After a year there, he was apprenticed to a local foundry owner. In keeping with the custom of the time, he had to supply his own tools. Part of the little pay he earned was left on deposit with his employer as a pledge of good conduct, to be drawn only at the time of an annual reckoning. But his first employer went broke, and William lost the better part of a year's wages. He completed his apprenticeship at another foundry. Wearing the traditional "freedom suit" that came with his graduation, he set out in search of a job. Wherever he worked, he managed somehow to send a part of his pay home to his mother.

In 1852, at the age of twenty-four, he married fifteen-year-old Amelia Thomas, and the young couple set up housekeeping in Philadephia. William was, his brother

20

WILLIAM H. SYLVIS

noted, a "kind and attentive" father, an "affectionate" husband. His spare moments were devoted to reading — he was deeply interested in politics and political economy — though his brother complained that his letters showed "a lamentable deficiency in spelling and grammar." His wages "scarcely provided" for the needs of his rapidly growing family. They had provided even less in recent months, for Sylvis had been laid up by burns he suffered when hot iron had been accidentally poured into his boot.

It cost about $10.57 a week then to support a family of five, the New York *Tribune* estimated. And it was no generous budget. After providing food, clothing, rent and fuel, it allowed twenty-five cents a week for furniture and utensils and wear and tear, along with twelve cents (of course) for a newspaper. Editor Horace Greeley wondered: ". . . have I made the workingman's comfort too high? Where is the money to pay for amusements, for ice cream, puddings, trips on Sunday up and down the river, in order to get some fresh air; to pay the doctor or apothecary, to pay for pew rent in the church, to purchase books, musical instruments?" A bricklayer at the time made about $1.88 a day, a carpenter or painter about $1.74, a plumber $1.90.

Molders had attempted to organize in the 1830s, but they could not maintain their union in the face of the widespread unemployment, the wage cuts, the business failures that were part of the panic of 1837. These recurring "panics" — later they were labeled "depressions" or "recessions" — were especially bitter to workingmen. They were thrown out of work at a time when jobs were hard, often impossible, to find. Neither their skills nor the few tools they owned could produce a livelihood for their families.

Help was often a matter of reluctant charity; hunger and hardship moved in for a long stay. Then slowly, business improved, and men went back to work. In the 1840s, when times were better, some molders had tried again. Others had experimented with the idea of cooperative ownership — the workers themselves were the owners of the foundry as well as its employees. They shared the profits — if there were any — as they shared the work. The cooperative foundries usually ended either in failure or in individual owners taking them over.

Sylvis had experienced the problem created by the expanding market. He had seen one employer reduce wages so he could put a lower price on his product. Other employers paid lower wages and offered lower prices. Then the first employer would ask — or demand — even lower wages so he could offer still lower prices. If the men objected, Sylvis observed, "a guillotine had been prepared and their heads immediately dropped into the basket." Sylvis had also seen the making of stoves broken down into simple tasks. Each man made only a single piece, needing little skill to do it. Wages fell so low that, even by stretching the hours of work, a man could scarcely obtain the "plainest necessaries of life."

Despite its defeat in the strike of 1857, the Philadelphia union managed somehow to survive. Secretary Sylvis was an active and vigorous member. He had "his say," his brother noted, on whatever came before the union. Largely at Sylvis' instigation, the Philadelphia union called a convention of molders' unions. As a result, in July, 1859, thirty-five delegates representing twelve local unions met in Philadelphia to discuss the organization of a national union of molders.

Sylvis later recalled: "No definite plan was formed. . . .

Nor was it possible to divine what the great objects of such an organization should be. A grating wrong existed, which it was necessary to remove and all felt the necessity of action." The inexperienced men exchanged ideas, discussed "crude" proposals, but could settle on no policy except to meet again in six months. But Sylvis was confident: "A great start was made and men began to think for the first time in their lives."

Sylvis was chosen to draft a message to molders; his handiwork in time became the preamble of the molders' constitution and was copied by a number of other labor organizations. It was a fervent appeal not only for a decent wage but for a place in society: "What place are we as mechanics to hold . . . ?" he asked. "Are we to receive an equivalent for our labor sufficient to maintain us in comparative independence and respectability, to procure the means with which to educate our children and qualify them to play their part in the world's drama; or must we be forced to bow the suppliant knee to wealth and earn by unprofitable toil a life too void of solace to confirm the very chains that bind us . . . ?" There could only be one answer, he declared: "In union there is strength and in the formation of a national organization, embracing every molder in the country, a union founded upon a basis broad as the land in which we live, lies our only hope. Single-handed we can accomplish nothing, but [and these are familiar words] united there is no power of wrong we cannot openly defy."

The delegates met again in January, 1860. Sylvis was proposed for the presidency but was defeated. Instead he was elected treasurer. As treasurer, he told the next year's convention that the union had spent over five thousand dollars the year before on strikes. The delegates promptly resolved that "strikes were to be discountenanced until every other remedy has been tried and failed." The union was by then, according to the Cincinnati *Daily Enquirer,* "the largest mechanical association in the world."

The dark shadow of civil war hung over their deliberations in 1861. Sylvis shared the view, common among working people, that the critical point was to preserve the federal union. He advocated a compromise plan to prohibit slavery in the North, protect it in the South, allow new states to decide for themselves. Sylvis chaired a convention in Philadelphia intended to rally support for efforts to stop the onrush of war. He served on a committee of 34 to carry on the campaign. But these efforts ended when Fort Sumter was fired on. Northern wage earners, Sylvis included, threw their support to Mr. Lincoln.

Sylvis helped recruit a company of molders for Mr. Lincoln's army, but, on his wife's insistence, he himself withdrew. One Philadelphia union adopted a motion that "this union stands adjourned until the Union is safe or we are whipped." A local of the typographical union disbanded because so many of its members had taken up arms. They were not alone; many unions enlisted in a body, many suspended activities during the war. Sylvis helped to recruit a second outfit when Confederate forces threatened Washington, D. C. When the threat eased, the unit was released, and Sylvis returned to Philadelphia.

At the start of the war, unemployment climbed rapidly and wages fell. But the demands of the war on the economy soon forced prices up. Two dollars, one labor leader later noted, would not buy what one had bought before the war. Employers raised wages only when workers began to protest. Soon, too, the demand for workers exceeded the supply. Unions revived and demands for higher wages broke out. In 1863, two new national unions were formed, four in the following year. *Fincher's Trade Review* exhorted the workers: "Organize. Organize. Organize in every village and hamlet, and become tributary and auxiliary to district, county, state and national trade organizations." The *Review* counted 79 unions in twenty trades in December, 1863; 203 unions in forty trades six months later; 300 in sixty-one trades by November, 1865.

The molders did not meet in 1862. They convened in January, 1863, though, and their first act was to elect Sylvis president. Under him the national union took on new shape, pioneering many union practices. Sylvis installed an annual system of finances, based on annual dues and the sale of union cards and charters. He set up a card index of the membership at the national office. He insisted a man must clear his debts with one union before he could transfer to another. He insisted, too, that all strikes must be authorized and that the national union would support only those that were. "Don't strike," he advised local unions, "until you are well organized, and then strike hard."

Sylvis quit the trade and went to work full time for the union. He persuaded his Philadelphia union — now Local 1 — to advance him a hundred dollars and he set out on what he called a "tour of experiment." He relied on local unions to take care of his food and lodging and to raise money to keep him on the road. In a year's time, he organized eighteen new unions, reorganized sixteen, placed twelve on a firmer basis. His total expenses for his trip of some ten thousand miles came to $899.86 — just seventeen cents more than had been raised. He noted that he had paid his wife $108; bought schoolbooks, $3.10; shoes, $10; clothes, $18.75; house rent, $25. Other expenses

included $2 in taxes, $6 in dues. Though he spent $58.90
for clothes, his brother later wrote: "He wore clothes
until they became quite threadbare and he could wear
them no longer . . . the shawl he wore to the day of
his death . . . was filled with little holes burned there by
the splashing molten iron from the ladles of molders in
strange cities, whom he was beseeching to organize." More
than once he begged a ride on an engine when he had
no money to pay his fare.

The 1864 convention reelected him and gave him a
salary of six hundred dollars a year. "From a mere pigmy,"
he told the delegates, "our union in one short year has
grown to be a giant; like a mighty oak it has grown up
in magnificent proportions with its giant branches stretching out in every direction, reaching into every corner of
the continent where our trade is known." These were the
happiest times of his life, he said. "I love the Union cause.
I hold it more dear than I do my family or my life. I
am willing to devote to it all that I am or have or hope
for in this world."

The union reached new heights in 1865 but the end
of the war faced it with critical problems. Trade collapsed
and unemployment spread. That summer, according to one
leader, "saw four millions of men standing where there
was room for but two millions; dull times were coming
fast, distress was making itself felt in many places. . . ."
Foundry owners set out to cut wages, organizing themselves into associations in some places for the purpose. At
one time, they were battling ten local unions in lockouts
or strikes. But the newly formed employer associations did
not always hold together; somehow, the union held
on.

Now Sylvis saw what, to him, seemed a new hope.

Trade unions, he said, are "only the first great step on the road to emancipation." The next great step would be cooperatives. In the cooperative foundries, as Sylvis foresaw them, the workers would own and manage their own business and share equally in its earnings. Cooperatives, Sylvis argued, would end the evil of working for wages; instead, the profits would be divided among those who produced them. With Sylvis' help, a cooperative foundry was organized in 1866 when the union's members in Albany and Troy were locked out. Its success inspired Sylvis to call for more. He predicted a thousand cooperative foundries would provide havens for the "storm-tossed toiler." Within two years, eleven had been formed. But they had little capital to buy materials and machinery, no bank would lend them money, they knew next to nothing about management and they had no access to the marketplace. Soon the cooperative foundries faded from the scene as outright failures or were turned over to individual, private owners.

Sylvis, meantime, had set out on still another road. In 1866, he met in New York with William Harding, president of the Coach Makers International Union, and Jonathan Fincher, secretary of the Machinists and Blacksmiths and editor of the *Trade Review*. They agreed to call a meeting of national unions to discuss forming a nationwide federation — a national trade union center. With the help of the Baltimore Trades Council, the national labor convention met in that city on August 20, 1866. A banner over the auditorium welcomed "the sons of Toil, from the North, South, East, and West." Delegates representing some sixty organizations — trades assemblies, national unions, eight-hour leagues, labor reform groups — took part. They were, the New York *Tribune* reported, "the intelligence, education and enterprise of the workingmen." The labor congress marked "an era in our history." The convention urged workers to form trades unions; it deplored strikes. It decided that each locality should determine its own form of political action. Most of all, it focused on the eight-hour day.

Sylvis was ill and unable to attend the Baltimore convention. He thought the results useful but he also noted that the convention failed to establish effective machinery to operate the organization, which had been named the National Labor Union. The delegates built a "splendid" railroad, Sylvis commented, "without providing wood and water to get up steam." But it did set in motion an agitation for shorter hours that reverberated across the continent until it was silenced by the depression of the 1870s.

The 1867 convention of the National Labor Union fell into a sharp argument over greenbackism. Sylvis again argued that trade unions were not enough, that they could not accomplish "permanent reform." It could be accomplished, he contended, only through the government issuance of paper money — greenbacks. Money must be made cheap, for cheap money would encourage investment in machines and materials. It would keep prices from falling and keep jobs plentiful. Money must be safe and convenient. Government would be the only lender and it would make loans at low rates of interest. Control of money and credit by the rich would be ended — "this power," he argued, "is blasting and blistering everything it comes in contact with."

In the following year, the status of women came in for heated discussion. The credentials of three women delegates were accepted but those of the woman suffragist

Elizabeth Cady Stanton were challenged. Sylvis defended her: she "has done more than anybody I know to elevate her class and my class, too, and God knows they need elevation." The convention voted to accept her credentials but not "her peculiar ideas."

The status of the Negro was debated, as it had been the year before. The Negro was no longer a slave, Sylvis argued, but he was not free. He had merely exchanged one form of slavery for another. Now they were all slaves together. The object of labor reform, he insisted, must be to eliminate slavery in every corner of the land. The convention avoided a decision because of "so wide a diversity of opinion among our members."

In 1868, Sylvis was elected president of the National Labor Union. In the following spring, accompanied by Richard Trevellick of the Detroit Trades Assembly, he set out on a tour of the former Confederate states. He invited Negroes to attend their meetings, to join in the common cause. "We will have the power," he said, "in this part of the country that will shake Wall Street out of its boots."

Suddenly, in the summer of 1869, Sylvis was taken ill. Four days later, at the age of forty-one, he died. The National Labor Union proposed a memorial for its president, but nothing came of it. Later, the Iron Molders International Union raised a monument to him. On it they put the words "Labor's Champion."

The National Labor Union continued to meet for several years. Some delegates insisted workingmen should have their own political party; others maintained political action would be most effectively carried out through existing parties. In time the National Labor Union split; it became a purely economic or industrial body. A National Labor Party was formed by the political activists. Both soon faded away. Only seven men were present at the last meeting of the National Labor Union in 1872.

One labor historian called it "a typical American politico-reform organization, led by labor leaders without organizations, politicians without parties, women without husbands, and cranks, visionaries, and agitators without jobs." In good measure, that was true. But it was also a major, if awkward and fumbling, effort to establish a national trade union center. The time was not yet ready, but Sylvis had pointed the way.

CHAPTER THREE

Terence Vincent Powderly

"An injury to one
is the concern of all"

"**B**ORN without previous notice, and when I wasn't expecting it," Terence Vincent Powderly philosophized many years after, "I didn't note the date until reminded of it later. With defective vision to start with I didn't see many of the bad or cruel things transpiring around me. I began to catch things early. The first was scarlet fever, after that some measles; the former deprived me of the use of one ear; in consequence, I did not hear half of the disagreeable things that others had to listen to. I was born of poor but Irish parents and that made up for a whole lot."

Before their marriage, Powderly wrote, "my father and mother were Terence Powderly and Madge Walsh; after marriage they were one, and I always held to the belief that my mother was the one."

Soon after his marriage, the senior Terence borrowed a gun, marched through the gateway of an Irish nobleman's estate, and shot a hare. He was convicted on three counts: carrying firearms without legal warrant, trespassing on a gentleman's estate and willfully taking the life of a hare.

He was sent to jail for three weeks. On emerging he said to his wife: "Let us leave this damn country and go to America where a man may own himself and a gun, too, if he wants to." The young couple crossed to Canada, stopped briefly in New York, then settled in Pennsylvania. There Terence Vincent was born — "as it was afterwards told to him" — on January 22, 1849.

He later complained that there were no child labor laws in his day — had there been, he was sure, his mother would have repealed them. She put him to work the first day he was able to do anything — with no allowance, he mocked, for overtime. His first paid job was tending switch on the Delaware and Hudson Railroad when he was thirteen. When he was seventeen, he was apprenticed to a machinist. Laid off three years later, in 1869, he traveled the machine shops and mines of Pennsylvania looking for work. At the time Powderly was working at Dunmore, a mine explosion at nearby Avondale killed several hundred miners. There, in a memorial service for the dead, he heard John Siney, head of the Miners and Laborers Benevolent Association. Standing on a desolate hillside, against a moss-grown rock, Siney talked grimly of life and death in the mines. "You can do nothing to win these dead back to life," Powderly remembered him saying, "but you can help me to win fair treatment and justice for the living men who risk life and health in their daily toil."

Powderly set out to find the union of his trade. When he did, he helped to organize Local 2 of the Machinists and Blacksmiths Union at Scranton, Pennsylvania. He soon became secretary, later president. Thus he was the first to be fired when the depression of 1873 struck. Again he took to the road in search of work. He found other jobs, but the blacklist quickly caught up with him. It identified

33

TERENCE VINCENT POWDERLY

him (and others) as active unionists, and therefore undesirable. He was promptly fired. Often he went hungry.

In 1874, while attending an antimonopoly convention, he was initiated into the strange and secret world of the Noble and Holy Order of the Knights of Labor. From that moment, Powderly wrote, "I knew no waking hour that I did not devote, in whole or in part, to the upbuilding of the Order."

In the year 1869 — it was the year of William H. Sylvis' death, the year in which Powderly had heard Siney on a desolate Pennsylvania hillside — a group of garment cutters in Philadelphia began to plan the organization that became known as the Knights of Labor.

These men had belonged to a garment cutters' association formed in the early years of the Civil War. The cutters had lost interest; many had moved west. The association became purely a benevolent association, providing benefits for sick or disabled members. By 1869 it seemed to have outworn even this limited use.

During a walk one Sunday afternoon, two of the men — Uriah S. Stephens and Henry L. Sinexon — agreed that the association had reached the end of its rope. They also agreed to do something about it. Each Sunday, then, they met in the park, moving several benches together to form a triangle. There, they and half a dozen others discussed the shape and substance of a new organization. Out of their discussion came Assembly No. 1 of the Knights of Labor — the first and parent assembly of what became, in its time, the largest labor organization in the nation's history.

The key architect was Stephens. Born in 1821, he had prepared for the Baptist ministry, but the panic of 1837

35

cut short his plans. Instead he became a tailor. He traveled to Central America, then on to California, returning to Philadelphia in 1858. In 1862 he helped to form a garment cutters' union to fend off a wage cut, and he became a prime mover in bringing the Knights of Labor to life in 1869.

The men felt a deep, urgent need for extreme, inviolate secrecy. They were convinced that open association exposed the members to "the scrutiny, and in time, the wrath, of their employers." They feared the possibility, a leader of the Knights said later, "of desperate men gaining admission for treachery."

Their new association welcomed men of almost every calling — except bankers, lawyers, doctors and those who sold liquor. (Later, doctors were admitted, but professional gamblers and stockbrokers were added to the list of exceptions.) At the start, new members were welcomed into Assembly No. 1 as "sojourners." They remained there only until there were enough of a similar trade or interest or industry to form their own assembly.

Admission into the order carried a heavy religious overtone. The prospective member was brought into an anteroom ostensibly for some other purpose. There he was asked if he believed in God, if he earned his bread by the sweat of his brow, if he were willing to take a solemn vow of secrecy. If a man refused at this point, he was turned away, often without ever learning why he had been brought there. If he agreed, he was taken into the inner room and initiated into the secrets of the order. He was told how the order offered protection against persecution and wrong, how the order combined its members against the hate and greed and self-interest of others, how it sought favorable public opinion and justice for labor.

The order would use every means to obtain and hold jobs for its members; it would provide aid in case of accident or misfortune. Without approving strikes, it would, nevertheless, if necessary, protect and aid its members. It would "extend a helping hand to all branches of honorable toil." The initiate was then instructed in passwords and signs. The name of the order was never to be used in public, nor its methods or objects revealed. If necessary, it was referred to simply as the Five Asterisks or Five Stars, thus: * * * * *

Heavily encumbered by secrecy, the progress of the Knights was slow. A few local assemblies were formed; in 1873, a few local assemblies were brought into the first district assemblies. By the latter part of the 1870s, there was growing talk of national organization, and enough local and district assemblies to justify it. In 1877, the anger and discontent of working people exploded in a "great upheaval," especially in the sweeping railroad strikes of that hot summer. The strikes were put down, often with violence. The strikers were blacklisted and forced to hunt new jobs. Their unions were trampled in the dust. The unsuccessful strikes scattered loyal members – and with them, the gospel – of the Knights of Labor to new sections of the country. The Knights' veil of secrecy and their call to solidarity proved attractive to many good union men. Finally, in 1878, in Reading, Pennsylvania, a convention of local and district assemblies organized the General Assembly. It was made the national governing body of the Knights. For the first time, the order adopted a declaration of purpose and principles. These it borrowed in large part from an extinct labor group called the Industrial Brotherhood. The order called for making "industrial and moral worth, not wealth" the measure of men.

It would seek "to secure to the workers the full enjoyment of the wealth they create; sufficient leisure in which to develop their intellectual, moral and social faculties; all of the benefits, recreations, and pleasures of associations; in a word, to enable them to share in the gains and honor of advancing civilization."

The General Assembly chose Uriah Stephens as its first Grand Master Workman. It adopted a motto, which, of all the heritage left by the Knights, has perhaps been the most (though often inaccurately) remembered: "That is the most perfect government in which an injury to one is the concern of all." It was said to have come from the writings of Solon, the Greek lawgiver.

"The Knights started on their national career in 1878," writes labor historian Norman J. Ware, "with a brave platform, but for a long time it was impossible to discover what they were doing. They were in sympathy with everything and involved in nothing."

Grand Master Workman Stephens resigned in 1879, and the General Assembly chose Terence Vincent Powderly to succeed him. For the next fourteen years he reigned over the order, over its greatest successes and its most abject failures. Under him, Ware goes on, "the Order changed from weakness to strength, from an insignificant handful to a prominent mass, from defense to aggression, and from ideas of brotherliness and mutual aid to revolutionary ardor." But the order never found a true direction. It never overcame the confusion in its purpose or the uncertainty about its tactics. It climbed to heights never before reached by an American labor organization, then fell back to extinction.

To John Swinton, a contemporary labor editor, Powderly seemed out of place. He was a slender man, with a drooping moustache and long, brown hair swept back until it almost reached his coat collar. He was surrounded, Swinton wrote, by "strapping big fellows with hands and shoulders formidable to the eye, unpolished gems in the main. English novelists take men of Powderly's look for their poets, gondola scullers, philosophers and heroes crossed in love but no one ever drew such a looking man as the leader of a million of the horny-fisted sons of toil."

He was a temperamental man, not physically strong, with a deep aversion to travel and a fierce hatred of liquor in any form. At one point he stayed on as head of the order only with the understanding that he would not be required to visit any local groups. But the very next year, the General Assembly raised his pay and instructed him to spend at least sixteen weeks on tour. Even then, he had only begun his trip when he was "overtaken by quinsy" and rushed back home. He announced flatly that he would speak at no more picnics where "the girls as well as the boys swill beer." He protested the burden of work, the invitations to speak, the banquets and the entertainments. "The position I hold is too big for any ten men," he complained. "It is certainly too big for me."

Powderly was an effective and often powerful speaker. He proved repeatedly his ability to move men. He was intelligent, with a natural dignity. When he was introduced to James McNeill Whistler, the famous painter eyed him through a monocle. "A beastly lot, your iron workers and miners," he shrugged. Powderly turned to a friend and, in what he insisted was his "sweetest" voice, asked, "Did you say this man is a painter? House or sign?"

Even before his election as Grand Master Workman, Powderly launched a fight to lift the order's heavy cloak of secrecy. Finally, though hesitantly, the General Assembly agreed to allow local and district assemblies to use the name of the order in public. No member's name, however, could be used without his consent.

Even more drastic changes were made in the course of Powderly's efforts to stave off the growing opposition of the Catholic Church. The word *holy* was stripped from the order's title; numerous scriptural passages were eliminated from the secret work (though much of the secrecy was retained); changes were made in the elaborate ritual. Powderly insisted the order's cause was just. If the Church was to align itself with wealth and oppression, he declared indignantly, he would take his stand with "God's poor." Even so, the Holy See was close to issuing a formal condemnation. Only the friendly intervention of Cardinal Gibbons of New York, persuaded by Powderly's arguments, prevented it.

The order met — and failed — one of its most crucial challenges in its own attitudes toward strikes. Powderly intensely disliked strikes. He laid down four rigid rules intended to insure a successful strike. A strike, he insisted, must be for a just cause. Every reasonable means must be used to avoid it. It must have at least an even chance of being won. Money must be on hand to support it. In Powderly's view, no strike ever seemed to meet his conditions.

A strike, Powderly maintained, was "a system of warfare." He said later that, though he had been responsible for the settlement of hundreds of strikes, he had never ordered one. Strikes were costly, he contended; lives were lost, homes wrecked, children deprived of education. They were "a great waste and loss." And yet, the Knights were involved in hundreds of strikes. Powderly insistently advocated arbitration and negotiation; employers just as insistently refused. Powderly found, as many union leaders found, that a strike was often the only answer. It was the only answer, too, to the hated "ironclad" contract, which forced a worker to renounce a union of any kind in order to get or to hold a job. All too often, a strike was the only way to improve wages or working conditions or reduce hours of work. It was the only defense against arbitrary wage cuts. Powderly could see the justice of strikes, but his distaste caused him to hesitate. He seemed never really able to make up his mind. His uncertainty was reflected in the Knights. It tried several times, for instance, to set up national strike funds, but it never succeeded.

In 1883, the telegraphers in the Knights prepared to strike Jay Gould's Western Union. Powderly argued vigorously in an effort to halt or delay it. His advice was ignored. The strike proved a disastrous failure. In 1884, though, the glass workers waged a victorious, five-month strike. Out in Denver, some Union Pacific shopmen struck spontaneously against a wage cut. The strike forced the company to withdraw the cut and to return the men to their jobs without penalty.

In the following spring, another Jay Gould line, the Wabash, announced a second pay cut in four months. The shopmen struck and were quickly joined by hundreds more on the Missouri Pacific and the Missouri, Kansas and Texas lines. Soon the walkout stretched the length of the Southwestern system, involving some 10,000 miles of track and 4,500 railroaders. *The New York Times* headlined its story: "A Revolt Against Low Wages on the Gould System." Even the "big four" brotherhoods of the operating crafts supported the strike. Powerful Jay Gould was forced to withdraw the wage cut. A few weeks later, the Wabash

41

reopened the issue. It laid off the Knights in its shops; they replied with a strike. They prepared, too, to call on Knights, wherever they worked on the Southwestern lines, to refuse to handle Wabash rolling stock. Again, Gould was forced to restore the strikers and locked-out workers to their jobs.

The victories over Gould gave the Knights a vigorous thrust. Gould had boasted he could hire "one-half of the working class to kill the other half" — that had been the key to his formula for enforcing low wages and long hours. Twice the Knights had outfought him — victories that over-shadowed equally critical losses, in the telegraphers' strike, in the strikes of Hocking Valley miners and Fall River spinners and others. But their successes caught the imag-ination of workers everywhere in the land. They flooded into the order by the thousands. In one year — from 1885 to 1886 — more than half a million workers joined the assemblies of the Knights of Labor. The numbers were so overwhelming that, for six weeks, Powderly actually halted recruiting. The Knights counted 729,000 members when the General Assembly met in 1886, but it might easily have been a million. Untold numbers of applications were never processed, hundreds of groups never chartered. "Never in all history," commented labor editor John Swinton, "has there been such a spectacle as the march of the Order of the Knights of Labor." For the first time in the nation's history, labor loomed as a significant, perhaps a major, influence. For the first time, organized workers had matched their strength against a giant cor-poration and had not been destroyed — had actually won. But even at that climactic moment, the Knights — and Powderly — hesitated.

In the year 1881, in the town of Terre Haute, Indiana,

a group of men, many of them dissatisfied Knights, had met to discuss the conflict that even then was developing between trade unions and the Knights. The group called for a national congress of labor in Pittsburgh, Pennsylvania, later that year. There was formed the Federation of Organized Trades and Labor Unions. A feeble organization, with little following, it struggled for five years to win the attention of unionists and to urge on Congress a program of favorable labor laws. But in 1884, this weak, struggling federation took the step that saved its life — and set unwittingly the course of the nation's labor movement for years to come. It bravely called for a general strike on May 1, 1886, in favor of the eight-hour day.

The very idea seemed to frighten Grand Master Workman Powderly. The proposition, he wrote, should be "discountenanced." He doubted that the workers of the country were educated to the shorter workday. He did not think a strike would be successful, that the date was a suitable one or the federation's plan a proper one. Many assemblies of Knights nevertheless began to prepare for the strike, mistakenly convinced that it had been ordered by their General Assembly. Powderly vigorously denied the General Assembly had acted on the proposal; he insisted it had nothing — and wanted nothing — to do with it.

When the day came, a rash of eight-hour strikes broke out. Knights, trade unions, anarchist and socialist groups — and mixtures of them — left their jobs to demand a shorter workday. Many of them succeeded. But in Chicago, tragedy struck. Police and strikers clashed on a picket line at the McCormick Harvest Works, and several strikers were killed. A meeting was called on May 4 in Haymarket Square to protest the police action and mourn the dead strikers. Thousands assembled under the watchful eyes of the

Chicago police — and of the mayor, too. The mayor soon left, convinced it was a peaceful affair and there would be no trouble. Suddenly, the police ordered the meeting dispersed. A bomb was thrown at the advancing police. Sixty-six were wounded; seven later died. The police opened fire on the crowd, and many more — the number is unknown — were killed and wounded. A wave of indiscriminate, unreasoning anger swept the country. All labor, lumped together into one faceless mass, was condemned as anarchistic, revolutionary, breeders of violence. New restrictions were demanded on unions and on union activities. The Knights and trade unions, though they had no connection with the event, recoiled under the heavy pounding. Powderly used every device to dissociate the order from the chain of events. He joined in condemning the eight anarchists who were charged with responsibility for the bomb, though no connection was ever established between them and the bomb. He refused to join in the many appeals for clemency, though many labor leaders, including Sam Gompers, did. "Better that seven times seven men hang," Powderly declared, "than to hang the millstone of odium around the standard of the Order in affiliating in any way with this element."

Uncertainty, too, marked the order's stand on cooperation. It remained in Powderly's day, as it had in Sylvis' time, a favorite panacea of many unionists. Some assemblies sponsored co-op grocery stores, sometimes housing them in their meeting halls. At one point, the order put money into a cooperative coal mine — and lost it. Powderly continued to insist on cooperation as the only escape from the "wage system." It was the answer, he claimed, to the worker's demand for a reward "commensurate with his dignity, his effort, his risks [and] his needs." But the order never seriously nor effectively put either its money or its members behind its professed belief.

Something of the same hesitance was reflected, too, in the growing conflict between the trade unions and the Knights. The order had no clear-cut policy — or, rather, it had several policies, frequently contradictory or ineffective. Some local assemblies were formed on strictly craft lines, such as Uriah Stephens' Assembly No. 1 of garment cutters. Others were mixed, though some of these passed on men of a particular craft or industry into craft or industry assemblies. District assemblies often resembled the familiar citywide trades union council, but sometimes they were centers only for several assemblies of a particular craft or industry. From time to time, the General Assembly agreed to issue charters to national craft assemblies; at other times, it discouraged them.

The trade unions had made an attempt to form a national organization in the Federation of Organized Trades and Labor Unions. By 1886, the effort was close to failure. At the heart of the attempt were Sam Gompers, Adolph Strasser and the Cigarmakers International Union. Around them raged a major battle in the war between the unions and the Knights.

A dissident group of cigarmakers, frustrated in its efforts to oust Gompers as president of Local 144, formed its own union, the Progressive Cigarmakers. It joined District Assembly 49 of the Knights of Labor. An ambitious, unruly and often radical assembly, D. A. 49 in time became a center of power and influence in the order. When Powderly linked his political fortunes with those of D. A. 49, the conflict with the trade unions became a certainty.

That summer, trade union leaders drew up a so-called treaty and submitted it to the Knights. It was a bold document that went far beyond the unions' relatively feeble power. The Knights rejected its demands. Powderly, the teetotaler, angrily denounced Gompers as being "too full for utterance" when the Knights and Cigarmakers sat down at the conference table. In fact, he added, he had "never had the pleasure of meeting with Mr. Gompers when he was sober." An irate Gompers charged Powderly with selling out to corporate wealth. He called the roll of defeats suffered by the Knights in recent clashes with employers. Invariably, Gompers angrily charged, the Knights simply sent the people back to work when the employers refused their demands. He said he wasn't charging Powderly with taking bribes, but a bribed man could have done the employers' work no better. That fall, the Richmond General Assembly — largest and most powerful in the order's history — rejected the efforts to reach an understanding with the trade unionists. That winter, the unionists formed a new trade union center — the American Federation of Labor — and put Sam Gompers at the head of it.

At that moment, too, the Knights clashed again with Jay Gould. This time, Gould drove the Knights off his Southwestern lines. The packinghouse workers in Chicago had won the eight-hour day in May of that year; they lost it that fall in a series of clumsy strikes. The Knights' membership began declining. In 1888 the order lost 300,000 members. The Federation soon caught up with it and passed it. The order never again was a major force in the labor movement.

In 1892, Powderly noted, Sam Gompers was the orator of the day at a trade union picnic in Powderly's home town of Scranton, Pennsylvania — where Powderly had once served two terms as mayor, where he had been its

46

only figure of national importance. In the parade that day, Powderly said, he would "occupy a place on the side-walk." In 1893, he was ousted as Grand Master Workman of the Knights of Labor. The order hung on, finally closing its last office in 1916.

Powderly could find no work in the machine shops; the blacklist took care of that. He won admission to the bar, but it brought him a poor living — he thought perhaps he was too soft in collecting fees. In 1898, President McKinley appointed him commissioner-general of immigration, and in 1902, President Theodore Roosevelt fired him. President Roosevelt reinstated him, though, a few years later when he concluded he had acted wrongly. Powderly remained in the federal service until 1921. He died in 1924.

CHAPTER FOUR

Sam Gompers

"The trade unions
pure and simple"

W HEN he was just ten, Sam Gompers was
put to learning the shoemaker's trade. Until
then, there had been a few short years of
reading and writing at the Jewish Free School, games in
the crowded, narrow, cobblestone streets of London's East
End, an occasional and prized visit to the theater (even
if it was only the "poorer" kind) and glimpses of distant
places in his grandfather's yarns. But Sam was the oldest
of the six children of Sara and Solomon Gompers, and
even the few pennies he could earn were needed at home.

As an apprentice shoemaker, Sam worked eight weeks
for nothing, then drew his first wage — about six cents for
a week's work. Like the men in the shop, he worked from
dawn to dusk. Low pay and long hours were common
enough in London, but Sam disliked the noise of the
shoemaker's shop. He persuaded his father to teach him
cigarmaking. Even the two of them, though, could earn
only a poor living for the family. With a grant from the
Cigarmakers' Society of London, the Gompers family
sailed for America. Among his memories of London, Sam

48

later recalled two in particular: the silk weavers of Spital-
fields, turned out from their jobs in the nearby mills, and
their cry, "God, I've no work to do. Lord, strike me dead —
my wife, my kids want bread and I've no work to do."
And he remembered that the workingmen of England
risked unemployment and hardship to support the cause
of the North and freedom against that of the South and
slavery. As he rolled cigars in the quiet of the factory,
Sam remembered, the cigarmakers sang of an African
mother and her son taken captive by a slave trader.
Another song told of the land "where a man is a man
if he's willing to toil and the humblest may gather the
fruits of the soil."

Sam landed at Castle Garden in the summer of 1863 —
in the midst of riots protesting the Civil War draft. Sam
and his father went back to work, at first as tenement
workers. They bought supplies from a wholesaler and
turned their finished cigars back to him. Sometimes they
were paid in scrip, which could only be exchanged at a
kind of company store for their needs. Sometimes the
wholesaler went out of business. Then they peddled their
cigars from store to store in an effort to recover something
of their investment in materials. Soon, though, Sam decided
to seek a factory job. He demonstrated his skill and was
put to work.

Cigarmaking in a hand shop of Sam's day was a quiet
operation. Only the casual conversation of the men or the
occasional click of the knife broke the silence. The men
sometimes sang, one of them alone or several together.
They paid one of their number to read aloud. While they
worked, the reader read from the day's newspapers, from
the economic and political writings of the times. They
discussed what they heard, argued the ideas of reformers

Library of Congress

SAM GOMPERS

and revolutionaries, talked of the things workingmen always talk about: wages and conditions on the job and slave-driving employers. So, bit by bit, Sam put together a picture of his adopted country and his place in it.

Sam became a member of the Cigarmakers' Union. On one occasion, though only a boy of seventeen, he spoke for the men in the shop in a quarrel with their employer. The employer scolded Sam — and the men: "You ought to be ashamed to be speaking for men old enough to be your father." But Sam insisted the men had a right to choose any spokesman they pleased. And he won an adjustment of their complaint. Sam soon found himself deep in the union's activities. With Adolph Strasser and other cigarmakers, he worked to strengthen their union. Their own local union was made up principally of skilled cigarmakers. Gompers and Strasser helped to organize the less skilled workers into separate unions. Later they brought them all together in one union, Local 144. Sam Gompers was made its first president.

Sam learned the trade of union leader from the ground up. He saw the union at work in the shop. He saw it push ahead, then fall back in the industry. He saw a handful of tenement workers emerge from their hovels in a strike for higher pay. The handful multiplied and was joined by factory workers until some fifteen thousand were on strike. The "revolt of the tenement workers" focused attention briefly on their miserable conditions. Money flowed in from Sydney, Australia, from London and from unions in many parts of this country. But the task of providing food and rent and medical care and clothing for the striking thousands finally proved too much, and the strike was lost. Sam was blacklisted. While he searched desperately for work, his family often went hungry.

Sam and his associates turned to building a strong, stable union, one that could stand up through good times and bad. They established strike funds and central reserves. They provided sick and death benefits for members. For the unemployed worker, they offered job information and travel loans. They lobbied for laws to end tenement cigar factories and halt child labor.

In the process, their ideas were shaped in the rough and tumble intellectual life in New York City. Gathered there were refugees from the great drive for human rights and nationalism that swept across Europe about midcentury. There were spokesmen for every kind of political and social philosophy. They saw workers organize in unions and political clubs and reform organizations. Sam had been an observer when police raided a demonstration of unemployed workers. A close friend was injured by a policeman's club; Sam escaped by jumping down a cellarway. Looking back, Sam saw in the tactics of radicals a barrier to normal, day-to-day activity and to smaller, immediate improvements. Radical tactics made the group a target of the main strength of society, he felt. These observations, he wrote, served him as guideposts for his future conduct.

Other craftsmen were also groping their way toward stronger, more stable unions. They, too, grappled with the problem of maintaining their unions on the job and on strike, in good times and bad. Out of the organizations they brought into being came a yearning for a national center, a national federation of trade unionists.

Gompers was chosen to represent the cigarmakers at a meeting of labor people in Terre Haute, Indiana, in 1881. He was ill, though, and unable to attend. But he was present later that year at a second congress that established a new national federation. Sam was the choice of many to head the new organization, but a false newspaper report that he was "the leader of the Socialistic element" wrecked his chances. He headed the committee that proposed it be called the Federation of Organized Trades Unions of the United States and Canada. Delegates quickly objected that the name would exclude unskilled workers and common laborers, who could claim no "trade." Sam explained that he did not want "to exclude any workingman who believes in and belongs to organized labor." He concurred when the delegates voted to name the organization the Federation of Organized Trades and Labor Unions. Its main job was to work for more favorable labor laws; Sam was one of five men chosen to direct its legislative work.

But the federation failed to take hold. Only 18 delegates turned up for the second convention; there had been 107 at the first. Attendance at the third was little better. Finally, at the fourth convention, in an act little short of desperation, the feeble, dying federation called on labor organizations throughout the country to establish the eight-hour day not later than May 1, 1886. Powderly vigorously opposed it; the workers were not yet educated to the shorter workday, he said. The Knights disclaimed any official interest in the proposal. But it caught the workers' imagination, Knights and unionists alike. When the day came, some 200,000 workers left their jobs in a strike for the eight-hour day. Many won shorter hours and many others won shorter workdays without striking. The movement was cut short, though, by the bomb that exploded in Chicago's Haymarket Square, splashing hate and anger over unions everywhere. The bomb not only killed the policemen, Gompers commented, "but it killed our eight-hour movement for a few years after, notwithstanding we had absolutely no connection with these people." The split over the eight-hour strike helped to push the conflict between the Knights of Labor and the trade unions toward a showdown.

The Knights had organized craftsmen in countless local and district assemblies. They also had a number of national assemblies, which were the equivalent of national trade unions, often in direct competition with existing trade unions. But the Knights were never able to make up their minds whether to encourage or discourage them. One faction rejected the whole notion of craft unionism, looking instead to broad, all-inclusive organizations that would take in small businessmen and farmers as well as workers. Another faction preached a stricter unionism, built around a particular craft or industry. In 1886 — the year of the order's greatest power — the General Assembly endorsed the antitrades union faction.

For many unionists, the contest had a direct and immediate importance. In Gompers' case, the Knights had thrown their support behind an anti-Gompers faction in Local 144 of the Cigarmakers. It had apparently defeated Gompers for the local presidency, but its candidate was ruled ineligible. The dissidents withdrew, and, with the blessing of District Assembly 49 of the Knights, formed the Progressive Cigarmakers. The Knights introduced a label to mark the cigars made by their members; the Cigarmakers sponsored their own union label.

Other trade unions complained that the Knights were "seducing" their members. They objected also to the Knights forming assemblies in opposition to existing unions. That summer — the year was 1886 — the trade union leaders drafted a proposed treaty to end their differences with the Knights. But their proposal would, in effect, have required the order to withdraw from competition with existing national trade unions; it would have been limited to little more than educational activities. Strengthened by a swelling flood of new members, with thousands more clamoring to join, the Knights spurned the treaty. In reply, they ordered cigarmakers in their ranks to choose between the Knights and the Cigarmakers' union; they could no longer belong to both, as many did. The rupture was further widened when Powderly accused Gompers of being drunk and Gompers heatedly charged Powderly with betraying his trust as a leader of labor.

In December leaders of the trade unions convened in Columbus, Ohio. The faltering Federation of Organized Trades and Labor Unions wound up its affairs and handed over its remaining funds — $287.04 — to a new organization formed the next day by these and still other delegates. Representing twenty-five organizations, with a claimed membership (the actual figure probably was half or less) of 316,469, the delegates launched the American Federation of Labor. They made Sam Gompers its first president at a salary of one thousand dollars a year.

Without waiting for his official term — or, for that matter, his salary — to start, Gompers went to work. He set up office in a little shed room loaned by Local 144. His desk was a kitchen table; he sat on an upended box. A neighborly grocer provided tomato boxes that a friendly carpenter converted into files.

Organizing was his major job — then and for years to come. He traveled wherever and whenever he could. His expenses were usually paid by unions in the towns he visited; he often made up the deficit from his own pocket. His first long trip carried him some ten thousand miles; he made fifty speeches in thirty-seven cities. He traveled on crowded, dirty trains, often packed with newly arrived immigrants en route to their new American homes. He traveled on freight cars, by boat, by whatever means were available. Wherever he went, he talked to workingmen — on the job, at factory gates, in the corner saloons that served as their clubs. He recruited volunteers to help with the job: local union leaders, an occasional minister, a woman or two were given honorary commissions as AFL organizers. Some were blacklisted, some driven out of town and many often went without eating. One wrote Sam that he was taking time off to go back to his regular job "to make a little money to support myself for a while." Another wrote that he had been living off the "charity of relatives and friends."

Slowly, workers were brought into existing unions or, in many cases, federal local unions — a local, that is, chartered directly by the Federation. When enough locals of a given craft or industry had been organized, Gompers would call them together and urge them to form a national or international union. In this way, he helped to bring into being international unions of boot and shoe workers, building service workers, carpenters, retail clerks, electrical workers, hotel and restaurant employees, musicians, street railway men, and many more.

There had been 25 organizations and 42 delegates at the 1886 convention. At the 1890 meeting, 103 delegates represented 83 organizations, with a membership conservatively estimated at about 250,000.

Under Gompers, the Federation called on the carpenters to lead a second fight for the eight-hour day on May 1, 1890. The carpenters' records show that shorter hours were won in 137 cities, affecting some 46,000 members. In 1892, the Federation attempted to rally national support for the besieged steelworkers at Homestead. Its call for a contribution of a day's pay, though, came too late to rescue their valiant fight. The American Railway Union in 1894 struck the plants of the Pullman Company, then declared a nationwide boycott of Pullman cars. The railroad managers, aided by President Cleveland, the army and the courts, smashed the dramatic uprising of the railroad workers. The workers asked Gompers and the executive council to call a general strike. The council refused; it had neither the power nor the authority, it said, nor would it be wise. Gompers and the Federation were (and sometimes still are) denounced for their failure to back the railroad workers with strong measures. They replied that the strike was lost, that a general strike would have served only to jeopardize needlessly the organizations and their members who responded to the call.

Sam served as a lobbyist and advocate as well as an organizer. The Federation was increasingly called on for advice and assistance. It raised funds to aid in strikes or lockouts. Sam served as an unofficial peacemaker in disputes between unions and was often called on to mediate disputes between unions and their employers. The constitution gave him little power. Basic policy was set by the convention. Beyond this, effective power was reserved to the international unions; each was an autonomous power unto itself. Gompers could only argue, beg, plead, cajole; he could neither dictate nor compel. His opponents derided Gompers' "voluntarism" — his emphasis on voluntary participation. One critic referred to the Federation as a "cross between a windbag and a rope of sand." But Gompers used this delicate "rope of sand" to build a vigorous labor movement and his own personal prestige as its leader.

These years of unceasing hard work and constant

debate sharpened Gompers' ideas about trade unions. More than ever, he became convinced that the trade union was not — as the socialists said, for instance — an instrument of revolution. It was an instrument of industrial peace. It was a tool for obtaining higher living standards, here and now — higher wages, shorter hours, safer, cleaner factories and workshops, better treatment, more education. "The ills of our social and economic system," he declared, "cannot be cured by patent medicines." The strike to him was no "relic of barbarism" as it was to Powderly. It was an important, socially useful weapon. The right to refuse to work was the final expression of a free man's strength. It was also a safety valve for the harsh workings of the industrial system — a natural outlet for anger and discontent. But the strike was to be used cautiously — only as a last resort and only after careful preparation. "Do not strike in haste," Sam warned, "and repent in leisure."

The preamble to the Federation's 1881 constitution had declared: "A struggle is going on in the nations of the civilized world between the oppressors and the oppressed . . . a struggle between capital and labor, which must grow in intensity from year to year and work disastrous results to the toiling millions." Gompers and his allies accepted the idea of conflict. They recognized that employers and workers competed for increasing shares of the product; their interests as a result were often far from harmonious. But they also believed that the gap could be bridged — by union contracts reached through collective bargaining.

The Socialists disagreed, and their rising strength gave their opinions some weight. To many of them, the trade union was the training ground for revolution, the "working class" the seed carrier of the revolution. Some Socialists contended the working class could accomplish the revolution only by political means — by voting itself into power. Others saw the trade unions as the base for both economic and political revolution. Gompers rejected both.

"I cannot and will not prove false to my convictions that the trade unions pure and simple are the natural organizations of the wage workers to secure their present and practical improvement and to achieve their final emancipation," he declared. His phrase, "pure and simple," ever since has identified his brand of unionism, both in pride and in derision.

When a delegate from a Socialist political organization presented his credentials to an AFL convention, Gompers opposed seating him. It was not because he was a Socialist, Sam insisted, but because he represented a political — rather than a trade or economic — organization. After long and heated debate, the convention upheld Gompers' stand.

An accumulation of Socialist anger and frustration, a severe depression that swept the country and a convention in the seemingly distant city of Denver, Colorado, combined in 1894 to defeat Gompers for reelection. He was returned to office a year later, though, after what Sam termed his "sabbatical year." He held the post, then, until his death some thirty years later.

Neither Sam's defeat nor his reelection ended the debate between him and his allies and the Socialists. He was attacked on petty grounds — they once accused him of smoking nonunion cigars — as well as on broad and fundamental issues. The Socialists continued to press for broader political activity. They proposed a legislative program including government ownership of industry that was heatedly debated and narrowly defeated in the convention of 1894. They objected vigorously to the participation of AFL

leaders with national business figures in the National Civic Federation. The Socialists claimed that the businessmen were using the labor leaders as dupes. Gompers and his associates insisted it was a serious effort to promote industrial peace and, at least, a useful sounding board for labor's viewpoint. The debate between Gompers and the Socialists helped to define and shape the program and the philosophy of what, in the end, became the mainstream of the American trade union movement.

On the opposite flank, Gompers and the AFL were targets of an equally sharp attack. It came from groups of employers who were organizing to oppose unionism of every kind at every step. The recently formed National Association of Manufacturers warned that the real danger "lies in the recognition of the union." Organized labor, cried a leader in the attack, is "socialistic — it knows but one law . . . the law of the savage." It was accused of endless crimes, blamed for every kind of trouble.

The National Metal Trades Association recruited non-union workers for its employer members, distributed blacklists, enlisted labor spies and strikebreakers and even supplied arms. The National Founders Association had been organized to negotiate with unions. It became the source of help for members involved in a strike; in time it became avowedly antiunion and open shop. Other employer associations provided labor spies to report on union activities inside their members' plants. The NAM, originally a trade association, became a spearhead of the attack on unions. It joined with a similar group in 1903 in the Citizens Alliance to launch a major open-shop drive. They explained that the open shop allowed men to belong to a union or not, as the men pleased. In practice, it came to mean that no union member would be employed, nor would the open-shop employer recognize or deal with a union.

The boycott, too, became a major target. It was a supplement to — or sometimes a replacement for — a strike, in which unions tried to persuade purchasers not to buy products made by strikebreakers or nonunion labor. Anti-boycott forces rallied behind the boycotted employers.

One such boycott was launched in 1902 against the firm of Dietrich Loewe and Company in Danbury, Connecticut, when it refused to unionize several departments in its hat factory. The American Anti-Boycott Association promptly promised the employer financial support. With this backing, the firm went into court demanding legal action against the union and the union boycott. It clamped legal claims on the homes and savings of union members just in case it was awarded the heavy damages it asked. In a stunning decision, the court awarded the employer $240,000 in damages. It made the individual union members responsible, along with the union itself, for paying them. No less seriously, the court decision invoked the antitrust laws to outlaw the union's boycott activities. The law had been passed to protect consumers and businessmen against giant trusts. But here it was used against a union of workers who had no other defense except their union. In the end, the Supreme Court upheld the decision. The AFL called on workers everywhere to donate an hour's pay to help the Danbury hatters. These funds saved their homes and life savings.

The Anti-Boycott Association struck again in the Bucks Stove case, this time nearly jailing Gompers and two of his associates. Metal polishers had struck the stove company in a dispute over hours of work and the firing of the union leaders. When the union declared a boycott against Bucks stoves, the *American Federationist,* official publication of the AFL, promptly put them on its "We don't patronize" list.

J. W. Van Cleave, head of Bucks Stove and president of the National Association of Manufacturers, demanded a court injunction barring the unionists from interfering with his business and from carrying out their boycott. In the few days between the time the order was announced and its formal issue, Gompers and Frank Morrison, secretary of the AFL, rushed an issue of the *Federationist* to press with Bucks stoves still on the boycott list. Sam added an editorial denouncing the firm's actions, relying on freedom of the press to protect his words.

The Anti-Boycott Association charged Sam with criminal contempt of court, along with Morrison and John Mitchell. As the nationally prominent head of the United Mine Workers, Mitchell had urged miners to vote a fine of five dollars on any miner buying a Bucks stove. The judge hearing the charges denounced the actions of the three men as "utter, rampant, insolent defiance" of the court order, a "coarse affront, vulgar indignity" to the court. Gompers lashed back. ". . . the freedom of speech and the freedom of the press have not been granted to the people in order that they may say the things which please," Sam told the court, ". . . but the right to say things which displease . . . the right to say things, even though they do a wrong." The judge sentenced Gompers to a year in jail, Morrison to nine months, Mitchell to six months. The dispute between the union and the firm was finally settled, and the Supreme Court dismissed the union's appeal from the injunction. In the contempt cases, the court found that too much time had passed, and the sentences were reversed.

The Danbury Hatters and the Bucks Stove cases dramatized the use of injunctions to fight unions. Such injunctions, labor men contended, often forbade men to do as a group the things they could do freely as individuals. Preliminary orders were often issued without even hearing the union side. Unions were compelled to prove their innocence, though even the worst criminal was assumed innocent until proved guilty. Even a temporary order that was later reversed or dismissed put the union under a handicap from which it often could not recover. Worst of all, in Gompers' eyes, the entire concept put a man's labor in the same category as a commodity. "You cannot weigh a human soul on the same scales on which you weigh a piece of pork," Sam declared. "You cannot weigh the heart and soul of a child with the same scales on which you would weigh any commodity."

Antiunion injunctions often rested on the antitrust laws, prohibiting combinations in restraint of trade. In fact, the Sherman Anti-Trust Act had been passed to prevent a combination of wealthy men from driving their competitors out of business and gaining monopolistic control of an entire industry. A combination of workmen seeking a raise in wages or improvements in their conditions was an entirely different kind of combination. These were never intended as — though in fact they soon became — a major target of the antitrust law.

The Federation's long campaign against the interference of courts in labor disputes — and especially the use of the antitrust laws to handcuff unions — reached a climax in 1914. The Democratic Congress took up proposals for revising the antitrust laws. One proposal was Sam's: a simple clause that provided, "The labor of a human being is not a commodity or an article of commerce." The idea was adopted. Labor organizations "instituted for the purposes of mutual help . . . and not conducted for profit" were put beyond the reach of the antitrust laws. So the Clayton Act of 1914 became, in the phrase of the day, "labor's Magna Charta," the charter of freedom for American workingmen. It failed in later years when courts interpreted the new statute. But it was, for that moment, anyway, in President Wilson's words, "a return to the primer of human liberty."

Some years before that moment, though, Gompers headed a delegation of labor leaders presenting President Theodore Roosevelt with labor's "Bill of Grievances." It called for an end to antiunion injunctions; for legislation to wipe out the sweatshop, prohibit child labor, fix an eight-hour workday; for free schools and textbooks; for compensation for workers injured on the job. The President listened carefully as Sam ran down the list, made some notes, thanked the labor leaders for coming. Speaker of the House Joseph Cannon, however, was abrupt. He terminated an angry interview in language that Gompers described as "lurid."

Labor had often campaigned for specific laws. It had frequently petitioned the government for a redress of its grievances. Gompers once took Roosevelt, then a young New York assemblyman, on a tour of tenement cigar factories and won his support for a law outlawing them. But unions seldom tried to organize union members as voters. They worked at politics in terms of issues, seldom in terms of men or parties. Now Sam proposed a change. He proposed that labor support men who endorsed labor

programs and goals and oppose candidates who were unfriendly. They would do so without regard to the candidates' party affiliations.

The policy was first put to the test in Maine in a
campaign against an unfriendly congressman. Sam carried
labor's case against Representative Charles E. Littlefield
to Maine voters. AFL organizers and local union members
planned and organized his tour. The Republicans countered
with their biggest guns — major national figures and administration leaders, including President Roosevelt himself.
Littlefield was reelected but by a substantially lower
margin. The Gompers campaign had helped him, Littlefield boasted. No other congressman, Gompers replied, had
asked for that kind of help. Successful or not, the Gompers
policy of rewarding labor's political friends and punishing
its enemies cut the pattern for labor's participation in
politics. One way or another, vigorously and indifferently,
effectively and clumsily, narrowly and broadly, labor has
followed that pattern ever since.

In the fall of 1917, with the nation at war, Woodrow
Wilson traveled from Washington to Buffalo to speak to
the AFL convention. To Gompers fell the "thrill of pride"
in introducing the first President ever to speak at a labor
convention. "The Presidential presence," notes historian
Thomas R. Brooks, "amounted to official recognition of
organized labor." In the immediate prewar period, as
during the war, Wilson looked to the labor movement as
a major supporter of his administration's war effort.
Gompers was made a member of the advisory commission
of the National Council on Defense. He worked out with
union presidents a program that claimed no less consideration for the industrial worker than for the soldier. He
got reluctant consent from industrial leaders — though by

no means from all — to maintain existing relations without change for the duration of the war. He negotiated an agreement with the War Department that recognized union wages and working standards in building army camps. The general principle was adopted in other areas of the government's war machinery. Under the pressure of rising prices and growing scarcity of labor, disputes arose over demands for higher wages. From the War Labor Conference Board came an imposing declaration — the first formal sanction for union organization and for collective bargaining to come from a governmental agency. Gompers, too, organized the American Alliance for Labor and Democracy in an effort to rally Socialist and radical support for the war and to offset radical opposition to the war.

Organized labor emerged from the war with its membership over the five million mark — more than four million in the AFL. It had won victories in wages and working conditions. It had achieved a sizable measure of recognition from the government and from industry. Gompers, himself, helped to construct the International Labor Organization as an instrument of the peace treaty. It was intended to unite nations around the world in working for higher living standards for workers everywhere. As it turned out, the United States itself did not become a member until 1934. The ILO still works toward these goals as an agency of the United Nations.

At the height of its power, pressed by a growing restlessness among workers, the Federation sponsored an organizing campaign among steelworkers. They flocked by the thousands to join the new union and they turned out in startling numbers on September 22, 1919 when the strike call came. But the steel corporations turned a deaf ear to President Wilson, to Gompers and the AFL, to the workers themselves. They counterattacked with a deafening campaign of confusion and suspicion and turned the strike into a rout.

There, perhaps, the dream was laid to rest. The AFL had been created by unions of skilled craftsmen. They had hoped to extend unionism to workers of every level of skill. Gompers had said, back in 1881, that no worker would be excluded. The Federation's very name embraced the common laborer as well as the skilled craftsman. Slowly, though, its focus had shifted. It had been battered on one flank by the Socialists, the anarchists, the Industrial Workers of the World, by endless radical groups. On the other, it had been assaulted even more heavily by the open-shop, antiboycott, union-hating employer organizations. It had often been denied the right to organize or to bargain collectively. The courts of the land had been used to break its strikes and disrupt its boycotts. The government had too often lined up with its enemies and backed their stand with troops. It had sought protection in the attitudes of the day, in hewing to a narrow, middle-of-the-road position that would call no attention to itself, bring no attack from the society of which it was — or wanted to be — part. It drew strength and security from the special and strategic skills of its craftsmen; it seemed to lose all interest in the plight of workers of lesser skills and in the growing ranks of the industrial worker. The latter had a different kind of skill — the skill of the assembly line, of the new machines, the new production techniques. The steel strike of 1919 reached out to some of these workers, and it was crushed. Craft unions became, and remained for some years, the fixed and dominant pattern in the Federation.

The dust of the war and the postwar turmoil had

scarcely settled when the country was hit by a jolting depression. It was coupled in the early 1920s with a widespread, intensive open-shop campaign under the label of the "American Plan." Labor's new millions wilted under the combined attack. The Federation was forced to yield ground.

In 1924, the Federation met in its annual convention at El Paso, Texas. It met, at the same time, in joint session with the representatives of Mexican workers. The meeting was a symbol of friendship between the workers of the two nations, for which Gompers had worked in recent years. When these sessions ended, Sam led a party of American labor leaders to Mexico City to take part in the inauguration of a Mexican president in whose success American labor — and Gompers particularly — had played an important role. Gompers fell ill. He was rushed back to San Antonio by special train, and there he died.

"Events of recent months," he had told that last convention, "have made me keenly aware that the time is not far distant when I must lay down my trust for others to carry forward. . . ." That convention became a song of praise for Sam, a tribute to his leadership. "We shall never stop," he responded to the tribute. "There are others who will rise and take our places and do as well, if not better than we have done." Once again, he summoned the fighting spirit of his younger years. "It is better to resist and lose," he said, "than not to resist at all."

CHAPTER FIVE

Eugene V. Debs

"That was only a cry.
That was pain"

A RETIRED Paris banker once mailed a postcard addressed only to "The best-loved man in all the world, now in Terre Haute, Indiana, U. S. A." It was promptly delivered to Eugene V. Debs. When Debs died, the Baltimore *Sun* mourned him as a "foolish, mistaken, exasperating, fine old man." The famous lawyer, Clarence Darrow, remembered him: "There may have lived some time, somewhere, a kindlier, gentler, more generous man than Eugene Debs, but I have never known him." President Theodore Roosevelt labeled him an "undesirable citizen." The Chicago *Tribune* called him, among other epithets, a dictator, an autocrat, a czar. An Ohio newspaper once described him as "the most dangerous and the most formidable enemy to law and order in the country today."

Eugene V. Debs organized one of history's most remarkable unions. It rocketed to a moment's prominence, then died a sharp and violent death. He campaigned five times for the presidency of the United States. The last time he ran from a cell in a federal prison and nearly a million Americans voted for him.

Gene Debs was born to Jean Daniel Debs, a poetry-loving, philosophic grocer, and Marguerite Marie Debs, known to her children as Daisy, a firm, yet gentle, loving mother. This closely knit, affectionate family lived in Terre Haute, Indiana, a raw-edged town on a high bluff above the Wabash River. There, with their last forty dollars, Daniel and Daisy had opened a small grocery store that earned them a modest living. There, on November 5, 1855, Gene was born. He was named Eugene Victor Debs in tribute to two greatly admired French authors, Eugène Sue and Victor Hugo.

Gene helped out in the family store when he grew up, though his parents were torn between the need for his willing and cheerful help and his open-handed generosity with the little store's stock of candy. He taught his younger brother, Theo, to fly a kite, build a raft, the ways of the Wabash as it rolled past the town. Most of all, in later years, Gene remembered the Sundays. Often, Daniel would hunt the nearby prairie, almost invariably returning with grouse or rabbit or whatever small game it offered. Daisy, with the true skill of a Frenchwoman, cooked a nose-teasing Sunday dinner. Afterward, the family settled down to listen as Daniel read from a favorite novel, an admired poet or a valued philosopher. "When I am away," Gene later told a friend, "every day seems alike, but when Sunday evening comes, I invariably feel something tugging at my heart strings." When Gene turned fourteen, it was decided that he would go to work. The growing family was an increasing burden on the little store. School seemed a tiresome repetition of the same old thing.

So in the summer of 1870, Gene went to work in the paint shop of the Vandalia Railroad at fifty cents a day. The boss handed him a scraper and put him to work

Labadie Collection, University of Michigan

EUGENE V. DEBS

cleaning grease off freight engines and scaling paint from railroad cars. One morning an angry engineer stomped into the paint shop. His fireman had shown up drunk, unfit to work, and he needed a replacement. He spotted the lean, sturdy, six-foot-two Debs. Almost before he knew it, Gene found himself in the cab of an engine, a coal scoop in his hands, facing a hungry firepit.

Firing an engine caught Gene's imagination. There was a sense of skill and power in feeding the hungry monster and maintaining a steady head of steam. But it was badly paid work. A man worked when there was a train to take out. He waited at the other end of the run until there was a train to take back. While he waited, he paid his own board and room. He worked before the run started, while the train was on the road and after it reached its destination. Hours were uncertain and wages were low — a fireman at the time might earn $1.25 to $1.50 a day.

It was dangerous work, too. Stray cattle, a washed-out bridge, a busted rail could derail an engine and wreck its cars. Tracks were new, often hastily and poorly built; they lacked the ballast and bed and steel rails that later made them safer. Engines, cars, equipment were often defective and had few safety devices. Trains collided with animals, with other vehicles and with each other. All too often, on the inevitable casualty list, the names of the engineer and fireman led all the rest.

Gene loved the work, but suddenly he quit. His mother had worried every time he left the house to take out a train. Somehow, though, she had managed to keep her fears to herself. One day, a friend of Gene's slipped under a locomotive and was killed. Gene's mother wrote him a desperate letter, begging him to give up railroading. Gene

72

was torn, but his affection for his mother won out. In October, 1874, he went to work as a clerk for a Terre Haute grocery firm.

His heart never really left railroading. He spent many spare hours around the yards or at railroaders' hangouts. When Joshua Leach called a meeting of locomotive firemen in February, 1875, Gene was one of the handful that turned out. Leach was grand master of the Brotherhood of locomotive Firemen, founded only two years before to help build a better life for the men of the craft. "My boy, you're a little young," Leach told Gene, "but I believe you're in earnest and will make your mark in the brotherhood." Later, Leach told a friend, "I put a tow-headed boy in the brotherhood at Terre Haute not long ago, and some day he will be the head of it." Just nineteen, Gene became a charter member of Vigo Lodge, Number 16, and its first secretary.

Gene was an active, vigorous union member. At the same time, he was deeply involved in the affairs of the Occidental Literary Club. Here he made his debut as a public speaker — a clumsy, fumbling, agonizing effort that left him hurt and embarrassed but determined to do better. The club, too, was host to a series of notable lecturers: Colonel Robert Ingersoll, a rising politician whose agnostic views and personal charm attracted sizable audiences; James Whitcomb Riley, the Hoosier poet who became one of Gene's close friends and who immortalized the warm-hearted Gene in one of his poems; Wendell Phillips, the abolitionist and labor reformer; Susan B. Anthony, the fiery suffragette whose meeting in Terre Haute was a total failure. In each, Gene found some measure of inspiration. His reputation in Terre Haute climbed steadily. In the fall of 1879, the Democrats proposed him for city clerk. Gene ran "away ahead" in the election and took office on January 1, 1880.

Meantime, he had been caught up more and more deeply in the work of the brotherhood. He had gone to its 1877 convention to make his first speech to a larger union audience. He and the other delegates were keenly aware of the sharp, violent railroad strikes that only weeks before had swept across the East and reached a climax of fury in Pittsburgh. Such strikes, Gene told the convention, could only mean "anarchy and revolution." Does the brotherhood encourage strikes, he asked. "To disregard the laws which govern our land? To destroy the last vestige of order? To stain our hands with the crimson blood of our fellow beings? We again say, 'No.' A thousand times, 'No.'"

The men who fought and lost the battles of that summer against strikebreakers and soldiers were blacklisted, forced frequently to seek other towns and other jobs. Membership in the brotherhood fell off, until only a handful turned out for the meetings of Vigo Lodge. Then not even a handful, only Gene. But he kept doggedly at it. He increased his contributions to the brotherhood's *Magazine* — news items, comments, even some clumsy verse — recruited new members, persuaded old ones to return. In 1878, he was made assistant editor of the *Magazine*. In 1880, with the fortunes of the brotherhood at low ebb, the delegates to the convention asked Gene to take the key job of grand secretary-treasurer and editor. He hesitated — other fields looked greener, his own future bright — but finally accepted.

He set up office in his mother's front parlor. His brother Theodore quit his job to become bookkeeper at ten dollars a week. His sister Emma left her teaching job and joined sister Eugenia as the office staff. Gene posted a ten-thousand-dollar bond to insure payment of the brotherhood's debts. Whenever he could get away from his duties as city clerk, he was off to meet with some of the "boys." Between trips, he sat at his desk night after night, writing letters, editorials, articles, handling the brotherhood's insurance claims and correspondence until he fell asleep from sheer exhaustion. Quietly, then, his mother turned out the light overhead and let him sleep. When his second term as city clerk ran out in 1883, Gene turned his full energies to the brotherhood.

One night in 1884, at the home of a married sister, Gene met a handsome young lady named Katherine Metzel. In the summer of 1885, they were married. She was the stepdaughter of a leading Terre Haute druggist. Her world of music, theater, romantic literature was a far cry from Gene's world of railroaders and unions and economics. But she learned to live in his world — his first gift to her was a bound volume of the brotherhood's *Magazine*. She gave him steady support and tender care in the rough times that were ahead of him.

In the same year, Gene was elected to the state legislature. He was determined to put through a bill requiring railroads to compensate employees who were injured on the job. Despite his hard work, the bill was finally torn to bits. Gene retired into an angry, resentful silence for the balance of the session. He swore to Theo that he would never again run for political office.

At the start, the brotherhood's main attraction had been a small insurance benefit for the widows and orphans of firemen who fell victim to railroading's many hazards. The brotherhood also hoped to raise the fireman's pay. It reasoned that if it gave the railroads "a class of honest and intelligent laborers, men upon whom they can depend, men who are equal in every way to the responsibility under which they are placed," it could ask for a com parably better wage. The 1879 convention decided flatly that it would "totally ignore strikes."

Tirelessly, Gene urged firemen to organize — and to urge other crafts on the railroads to organize. He traveled the roads in "rain, snow or sleet, half the night or till day-break," he told a friend. He was ordered out of round-houses and terminals by angry superintendents, put off trains while trying to "deadhead" to another stop. "I rode on the engine over mountain and plain," he said, "slept in the caboose and bunks and was fed from their pails by swarthy stokers who still nestle close to my heart. . . ." He sometimes left home with a suitcase or two, returned only with the clothes he wore. He gave away most of what money he had in his pocket to rail-roaders down on their luck. His salary, one biographer noted, was "a fund for indigent railroad workers." He often returned home exhausted and ill and discouraged. Kate nursed him to health again; he spent long hours in talk with Theo and with good friends. As long as they lived, Gene spent his Sunday evenings in Terre Haute with his parents.

Across the land, workers were organizing. The Knights of Labor in little more than a year recruited half a million or more. The trade unions, organized in 1886 in the American Federation of Labor, were gaining new strength. The brotherhood's 1885 convention, reflecting the spirit of the times, ended the long-standing resolution to "totally ignore strikes." It invited the Brotherhood of Locomotive Engineers to join hands "in all their grievances," but the engineers refused to listen. They would never cooperate with another union, their grand chief, P. M. Arthur, declared. The engineers would take care of themselves; other labor organizations would have to do the same.

From time to time, the two organizations cooperated in defending themselves against a wage cut or in jointly seeking a raise. More often, they — as well as the other railroad crafts — went their own way. Strike after strike was lost; strikebreakers quickly replaced the strikers, while members of other unions continued indifferently to work. Gene hoped this disastrous competition would end in the bitter, hard-fought strike against the Chicago, Burlington and Quincy. But the engineers sued for peace without consulting the firemen.

The rout of the CB and Q strike topped an already long list of lost battles. It convinced Gene that railroad workers must find the way to close, complete cooperation. Corporations band together, he reasoned, when they are attacked or when their employees ask for higher pay. Railroad employees need a similar federation. ". . . no time should be lost in forming an alliance," he wrote in the *Magazine*. ". . . For purpose of protection, the throttle and the scoop, the switch and the brake must be in close alliance and equally firm and defiant."

Gene energetically led the way, step by step, to such an alliance. In June, 1889, the firemen, the switchmen, and the railway trainmen formed the Supreme Council of the United Orders of Railway Employees. In September, the Brotherhood of Railway Conductors became the fourth member of the council. At first, the council's successes seemed to point the way to unity. Then a dispute broke out between the switchmen and trainmen over yard jobs on the Chicago and Northwestern. The council quickly ruled that the trainmen had "formed an alliance with the company" to take over the switchmen's jobs. But it split down the middle in attempting to set a penalty. By one vote, the council expelled the trainmen. With that act, it insured its own disruption. Soon after, it formally dissolved.

No longer did Gene fear the strike. Now he wrote: "The strike is the weapon of the oppressed." He explained: "Labor unions and brotherhoods are not organized for strikes any more than governments are instituted for war. But labor unions have striking power just as governments have war powers. . . . If such powers are surrendered, the result will be degradation and enslavement." He looked around him and saw the growing strength of the American Federation of Labor unions. He saw poverty on every hand, in sharp contrast to the growing wealth and power of the corporations. He had been impressed by the swelling ranks of the Knights of Labor. He puzzled long over the question, "What can workingmen do for themselves?"

Suddenly, at the height of his influence, Gene announced he would resign all the offices he held in the brotherhood. The delegates to the 1892 convention pleaded with him to stay. Finally, he agreed — but only as the editor of the *Magazine.* He said he wanted just nine hundred dollars a year salary; the convention promptly voted him a thousand.

Gene had started the E. V. Debs Publishing Company the summer before. It was said that he would go to New York to launch a national labor newspaper. Then, in the summer of 1893, he ended the speculation. Following a secret meeting in Chicago, he announced the formation of the American Railway Union. The new union, he pointed out, would open its doors to any railroad worker, from the lowliest yardman to the "aristocratic" engineer. A single union would end the ruinous rivalry between craft unions, he contended, and stop the railroads from playing one organization against another. One union, uniting the entire work force of a railroad, would reach nearer equality with the corporation that employed its members. The strength of all workers, he emphasized, would be put behind the rights and hopes of the least of them. Gene would serve as its president at a salary of seventy-five dollars a month.

The ARU would work for higher pay and better working conditions. It would lobby for more favorable laws for workingmen. It would provide cheap life insurance. The new union would not put up with "intemperate demands," but it would "protect the humblest member in every right he can justly claim." No strike would be called without approval by a majority of the workers directly involved. But when a strike was called, the full strength of the ARU would be behind it.

The first lodge was formed in August, 1893; within a few weeks there were three dozen. Men flooded into the union by the hundreds. By fall, eighty-seven lodges had been chartered and the ARU was established on several major systems and numerous smaller lines. Almost immediately it was put to the test. A court order in Denver forced a pay cut on Union Pacific workers. Gene rushed to the scene, bellowing angrily that the order was "a death blow to liberty." Under ARU pressure, the order was overruled, the pay cut restored.

Then it tangled with James J. Hill, the powerful and ruthless railroad builder of the Northwest. A strike swept over the western end of the Great Northern, moving relentlessly eastward until no wheel turned between St. Paul and the West Coast. Gene argued the strikers' case for a wage increase before a group of businessmen in the Twin Cities. He won them over, and they persuaded Hill to settle the strike. The businessmen's verdict put $146,000 more each month into the pockets of the Great Northern workers. As Gene's train pulled out of the yards at St. Paul after the strike, grizzled trackmen, shovels in their hands, lined the track and lifted their hats in salute. "In all my life," Gene said, "I have never felt more highly honored."

In the summer of 1894, some four hundred delegates, representing more than 100,000 railroad workers, met in Chicago in the ARU's first convention. President Debs sounded the keynote: "The forces of labor must unite. The dividing lines must grow dimmer day by day until they become imperceptible, and then labor's hosts, marshalled under one conquering banner, shall march together, vote together and fight together, until working men shall receive and enjoy all the fruits of their toil. Then will our country be truly and grandly free." The convention adopted resolutions condemning the use of troops to break strikes. It called on workers to support political candidates who agreed with their principles, regardless of party. Despite Gene's vigorous urging, they refused to open the door to Negro members. But these soon became side issues. The convention quickly focused its concern on the strike at the Pullman Company Works at nearby Pullman, Illinois.

The Pullman strike had broken out a month before. The strikers accused the company of firing several members of a union committee, despite the promise that no harm would come to any employee serving on it. In a larger sense, though, the strike voiced an accumulation of anger and humiliation and suffering in the months and years before.

George Mortimer Pullman's first sleeping car, "The Pioneer," had carried the funeral party accompanying the body of the martyred Abraham Lincoln from Chicago to Springfield in the spring of 1865. It was the forerunner of a long line of Pullman cars — sleeping cars, hotel cars, dining cars — that revolutionized rail travel. They made possible not merely overnight travel but travel in ease and comfort the width of the continent without changing cars. By 1894, Pullman — now the head of a wealthy corporation — was operating sleepers and diners over more than 125,000 miles of track. Some said it was one of "the most outrageous monopolies of the day."

In the late 1870s, Pullman built a great factory just south of Chicago and, along with it, a town to house its workers. He built big, comfortable nine-room houses for company executives and great barrackslike tenements for the workers. In these, five families shared a water faucet; two families, sometimes more, shared a toilet. He built stores, a hotel, a library. A single church was intended to meet the residents' religious needs. He barred liquor (except for hotel guests); he banned anything that could be described as a "baneful element," including saloons, union organizers and labor organizations. No man, of high state or low, could own an inch of Pullman land nor the smallest Pullman house. It was all part of the Pullman Company investment. It was a handsome town, some said, a "model town," "a veritable paradise." One newspaper reporter described it: "The corporation is everything and everywhere . . . the corporation does practically everything but sweep your room and make your bed, and the corporation expects you to enjoy it and hold your tongue."

A sharp, biting depression swept across the country in 1893. Countless workers lost their jobs; countless others had their wages cut. At Pullman, the work force fell from 5,816 in midsummer to 2,000 by November — and many of these worked part-time. "We tried to give all of them some work," a vice-president explained. Cutting wages, Pullman claimed, was the only way he could compete. He shut down the company's Detroit shops and moved the work to Pullman. He spent money on improvements. In his own view, he did all he could to help the company and its employees weather the depression.

But Pullman's view was a narrow one. The company lost $52,000 on its new car contracts that winter. The employees lost $60,000 in pay cuts. The company had ended its fiscal year in 1893 with profits of over $6,500,000. It paid its customary 8 per cent dividend and added $4,000,000 to its already huge surplus. In 1894, at the end of that bitter, depression-ridden winter, the company again paid its customary 8 per cent to stockholders and put another $2,000,000 in its surplus funds. Some employees had been laid off for weeks, even months; many worked only a day now and then; a few worked steadily at reduced pay. Hunger and even starvation were not unknown that winter in Pullman. When spring came, the Pullman employees formed local unions. Some questioned whether they were railroad employees, but they were, nevertheless, given charters by the American Railway Union. They asked the company to restore the wage cuts, to reduce the company-imposed rents, to cut company charges for water and gas. Pullman replied that wage-cutting had been necessary to maintain the company's new car-building business. (Its Pullman car operations continued without interruption or reduction in charges.) Nor could the company adjust the rents or charges for utilities. He explained that the town had returned a profit of only 3.8 per cent, instead of the expected

6 per cent. Moreover, the company's responsibility as a landlord had nothing to do with its responsibilities as an employer.

The committee of workers met twice with company officials. The men were assured that no man would be harmed for serving on the committee. They were also told flatly, not once but several times, that neither their wages nor the rents nor the utilities charges would be changed. The company agreed to look into the men's complaints about conditions on the job. Then three committeemen were laid off — inadvertently, the company claimed; in retaliation, the employees maintained. A strike was called, and by nightfall the great Pullman Works was shut down.

Only the energetic work of a relief committee, the help of the mayor of Chicago and various community groups staved off hunger and the outright starvation that soon laid hold of the residents of the "model town." The delegates to the ARU convention were told that food supplies in Pullman were running low; the situation was growing more desperate daily. "Act," a former Pullman minister urged the delegates, "in the name of God and humanity, act quickly."

The delegates sent a committee to the company; it was told the company would not deal with the American Railway Union. The convention sent a second committee, made up of Pullman employees. As far as the company was concerned, they were told, the strikers were no different from "men on the sidewalk." Pleas from civic groups, city officials and others were rejected or ignored. In anger and near desperation, the convention sent word that, unless the company agreed to arbitration, the American Railway Union would boycott Pullman rolling stock. It would call on its members, wherever they worked, to refuse to handle

Pullman sleepers or diners. A Pullman official shrugged it off. A boycott could not hurt it, a vice-president said, though it might injure the railroads and the general public.

The twenty-four railroads terminating or centering in Chicago were represented by the General Managers Association. They operated some 41,000 miles of track and were worth close to a billion dollars. "Gentlemen," the association was told, "we can handle the brotherhoods, but we cannot handle the American Railway Union. We have got to wipe it out. We can handle the other labor leaders, but we cannot handle Debs. We have got to wipe him out, too." The association insisted that the railroads had no alternative but to honor their contracts to carry Pullman equipment.

On the night of June 26, a few men refused to switch some Pullman cars. They were fired; other men quit in protest. The boycott spread like a prairie fire, to line after line, from Chicago to the West Coast. The general managers recruited strikebreakers in a dozen eastern cities. The brotherhoods — engineers, firemen, conductors — turned their backs; their men stayed on the job. But the Chicago yards were jammed with trains. The number of strikers climbed day by day — to forty thousand, some said, at the end of the third day (that was the day George M. Pullman left Chicago to spend the summer on the New Jersey seashore), to more than a hundred thousand by the end of a week.

Crowds — unemployed workers, curiosity-seeking spectators, women and children, as well as strikers and locked-out workers — were making life miserable for the railroads at the terminals and yards and crossings. The Chicago *Tribune* pictured "mobs" running wild. It cried that supplies of food and ice and meat were running low. The general managers warned, "In a few hours we will be in the midst of a reign of physical violence." The U. S. attorney in Chicago wired for approval to buy a hundred riot guns. Deputy marshals were sworn in and turned over to the railroads by the scores – they were later described as "toughs, thieves, and ex-convicts."

The Attorney-General of the United States, Richard Olney – a former railroad lawyer and a member of the boards of directors of several railroads – ordered the U. S. attorney and the U. S. marshal in Chicago to use every legal means to move the mail. Any train carrying mail, whether a single pouch or a carload, was a mail train, he said. Any interference with Pullman equipment usually carried by such trains could be considered interference with the mails. The general managers demanded that the government prosecute Debs, the ARU, the strikers. They called for sweeping court orders to shackle the boycott. Olney agreed. He appointed another railroad lawyer as his special representative to help carry out the plan.

Looking back, Gene described the situation as he saw it at the end of the first week: ". . . the general managers were as dead as a doornail. The strike was won. Not a wheel moved. Every railroad yard was as quiet as a cemetery. But at that time, the courts, the President and the Federal and then the State soldiers took a hand and the strikers were whipped out of their boots." What had started out as a dispute with the railroads, Debs said, became "a conflict in which the organized forces of society and all the power of . . . government were arrayed against us."

On the seventh day, the federal court issued a sweeping order against the strike. It charged Debs, his associates and the union with conspiring to disrupt interstate commerce and to interfere with the U. S. mail. Debs and other strike leaders were arrested but quickly released on bail. Debs seemed unworried. Injunctions can't move trains, he said. But, on the eve of Independence Day, President Grover Cleveland ordered federal troops into Chicago.

His action provoked an angry, outraged protest from Governor John Peter Altgeld of Illinois. The presence of federal troops in Illinois without the consent of the governor or of the state legislature was a violation of the U. S. Constitution, he said. The state militia was fully capable of meeting the situation; if railroads were not operating, it was because they could not get men, not because of violent obstruction. President Cleveland brushed off the protests. He suggested that the discussion should give way to efforts to "restore obedience to law and to protect life and property." He told a friend: "If it takes every dollar in the Treasury and every soldier in the United States Army to deliver a postal card in Chicago, that postal card shall be delivered."

The railroads were guarded, by then, by some 3,000 state troops, 3,300 police, 1,000 army regulars, 50 deputy sheriffs, 1,000 deputy marshals. Crowds heaved rocks at trains operating under guard and with crews of "scabs" — strikebreakers replacing the regular crews. Boxcars were overturned and switches jammed. At some yards, fires were set and scores of boxcars went up in flames. The general managers and most newspapers accused strikers of arson and robbery, of "a desperate and lawless fight." Debs pointed an accusing finger at the railroads. The ARU would move any train that did not include a Pullman. The soldiers were being used, he protested, to humiliate workers into obeying "the will of their oppressors." On July 8 President Cleveland issued an unprecedented warning to bystanders, spectators and strikers: Do not take any part in unlawful obstructions or assemblages. Those who fail to disperse will be regarded as "public enemies." Troops, he warned, cannot distinguish betwen guilty participants and curious onlookers.

Angered by the Pullman Company's defiance, by the state of near-martial law, trade unions in Chicago called for a general strike. Under their prodding, Sam Gompers convened an emergency meeting of the AFL executive council in Chicago. Debs asked the union leaders to proclaim a general strike. Short of that, he asked Gompers to carry a peace proposal to the general managers; he asked only that the men be returned to their jobs. The union leaders proposed Debs select any two members of the group to carry his proposal. Debs refused; he wanted only Gompers. The group finally issued a statement declaring that it had no power to call a general strike; that even if it had, a general strike would be unwise. It denounced "the gathering, growing forces of plutocratic power and corporation rule." It lashed the railroad corporations for violating laws for years yet demanding government aid when faced by labor.

Both the railroads and the Pullman Company were deaf to proposals for ending the dispute. Under the protection of thousands of armed guards, trains were moving again. By mid-July the first contingent of federal troops left Chicago. Almost at that moment, Debs and his associates were arrested a second time — this time on charges of violating the federal court injunction. This time, too, instead of accepting bail, they chose to stay in jail. For five days, they were out of touch with the strike. Perhaps the fight was already lost. But they themselves had accomplished what the general managers weeks before had set out to do: to remove the strike leaders from the scene.

Weeks later, the federal court heard the charges of contempt of court against Debs and his associates. It found the men guilty of violating the court injunction and sentenced Debs to six months in jail, his codefendants to three months. No sooner had the men started their jail terms than they faced the court a second time on charges of conspiracy. Under the pounding of Clarence Darrow, the railroad managers developed conveniently short memories; they could not recall what had gone on in their association meetings. George M. Pullman fled the city rather than take the witness stand. Debs took the stand, though, to underscore at length the peaceful, nonviolent intent of the ARU. Darrow insisted that the conspiracy charges were being used to hound men into jail merely for exercising their right to strike. Then a juror fell ill. The defense proposed several ways of continuing without him. The judge, however, rejected them and discharged the jury. The case was postponed several times, then finally dropped.

Debs and his fellow prisoners were given a large measure of freedom at McHenry County jail. Sheriff George Eckert allowed them to wear ordinary clothes, play ball in the street behind the jail, receive unlimited visitors and mail. They took their meals with the sheriff's family. Here, for the first time in years, Debs had time for thought and study. ". . . it was here," he wrote later, "that socialism gradually laid hold of me in its own irresistible fashion. Books and pamphlets and letters from socialists came by every mail and I began to read and think and dissect the anatomy of the system in which workingmen, however organized, could be shattered and battered and splintered at a single stroke."

The American Railway Union was shattered. Gene assumed personal responsibility for its debts, some $40,000 of them. Ultimately, he paid every penny. From this time on, Gene earned his living by writing and lecturing. On New Year's Day, 1897, he wrote the remnants of the ARU: "The issue is Socialism versus Capitalism. I am for Socialism because I am for humanity." In that year, too, the last convention of the ARU became the first convention of Social Democracy of America. In 1900, the Social Democrats nominated Gene as their candidate for President. Gene accepted with the proviso: "I am not fitted either by temperament or by taste" for the presidency. "If there were any chance of my election I wouldn't run." He campaigned for government ownership of the means of production. "The few who own the machines do not use them," he explained. "The many who use them do not own them." The result, he argued, was a few millionaires and many beggars, extreme wealth and abject poverty, "princely palaces and hideous huts, riotous extravagance and haggard want." He polled 87,814 votes. In 1904, when he ran as the candidate of the new Socialist Party, he drew over 400,000 votes. Four years later, he hired a private campaign train, dubbed the "Red Special," to make a "whistle-stop tour" of the country — an innovation in campaigns that later was copied many times by major party candidates. But his vote was hardly any larger. In 1912, though, a rising interest in the Socialist Party and a growing protest doubled his vote. He polled over 900,000 votes, some 6 per cent of the votes cast that year.

Meantime, Gene still maintained a lively interest in

unionism. Some Socialists contended they should try to capture control of the regular AFL unions. Gene argued that unions should be conscious, active advocates of revolution, their purpose to overthrow the system, not merely to raise wages. The Socialist Party would be the workers' voice in organizing the political revolution, industrial unions their revolutionary voice in taking over industry. In 1905, he joined a handful of radical leaders in calling the meeting that led to the organization of the Industrial Workers of the World. The IWW would build revolutionary industrial unions capable of taking over farm and factory, mine and mill for the benefit of the workers. Almost before it could get under way, though, three key leaders were kidnapped and jailed on charges of murdering Frank Steunenberg, a former governor of Idaho.* Debs plunged into an intensive campaign to arouse support for the arrested leaders. He exploded with an angry, fist-pounding editorial in the *Appeal to Reason,* a popular Socialist weekly. He challenged a statement that the three men would never leave Idaho alive. "Well, by the gods," Debs declared, "if they do not, the governors of Idaho and Colorado and the masters of Wall Street, New York, to the Rocky mountains had better prepare to follow them." He threatened: "If they attempt to murder Moyer, Haywood, and their brothers, a million revolutionaries will meet them with guns." Years later, challenged himself on how he could have sounded this call for a mob, he replied: "Oh, that. Why, my god, man, that was only a cry. That was pain." Haywood's trial ended in acquittal — Gene called it "the greatest legal battle in American history."

*See page 99.

But the Western Federation of Miners, weakened by the enforced absence of its radical leaders, pulled out of the IWW. It abandoned its commitment to socialism and moved into channels where Gene chose not to follow.

Soon the shadow of war lengthened over the land. Gene saw his friends who opposed American entry into the war sent to prison. He saw radical publications suppressed and mobs vent their anger against those bold enough to speak out against war — or sometimes only because the speakers were foreign born or spoke with an accent. Gene, too, spoke out and was arrested. So, in 1919, he began serving a term of ten years in prison. As Prisoner No. 9653 at the Atlanta, Georgia, prison, Debs mounted his fifth and last campaign for the presidency. His vote — 919,977 — was only a few thousand more than in 1912.

As a prisoner, he became convinced of the urgent need for a more humane prison system. His first work, after President Warren G. Harding pardoned him in 1921, was a series of articles and a book on prison reform. In the front of the book, he wrote his creed: "While there is a lower class, I am in it; while there is a criminal element I am of it; while there's a soul in prison, I am not free." He returned again to leadership in the frustrated and greatly weakened Socialist Party. He began publication of a newspaper. But in 1926 he sickened and died.

Back in Terre Haute, the president of the Central Labor Union came to Theo. He recalled how Gene had helped build the local Labor Temple. "You will have to give him to us for a while, Theodore. You know he belongs to us." There, in the Labor Temple underneath a bronze plate acknowledging his part in building it, his body lay in state.

CHAPTER SIX

William D. Haywood

"The Continental Congress
of the working class"

T HE Western Federation of Miners was born in an Idaho jail — the aftermath of a bloody and brutal battle between the miners and mineowners in Idaho's Coeur d'Alene. For the next ten years, open warfare racked the hard-rock mining districts of the Rockies. "Mines were blown up," writes labor historian Charles Madison, "men were murdered on both sides, strikers were herded in filthy bullpens or driven across state lines, and the rules of law and order were either repudiated or ignored by an arbitrary militia." Madison cites another historian: "The strikes in the mining districts of the West came nearer to real warfare than did any other contests in the history of the American labor movement." Out of the federation, out of the violence and oppression and bitterness came the Wobblies — the Industrial Workers of the World and William Dudley Haywood. He was a rugged, scarred, one-eyed mountain of a man. In the rough language and crude ways of a "quick-on-the-draw" frontier, he voiced the loneliness, the hurt, the anger and longing of the worker at the bottom of the nation's industrial pile.

Haywood was born in Salt Lake City in 1869 — the year

92

Sylvis died, the year Powderly heard Siney mourn the dead miners of Avondale, the year Stephens and his friends put together the Knights of Labor. His father, Haywood wrote, came from an old American family — "so American that if traced back it would probably run to the Puritan bigots or the cavalier pirates." His mother had come to Utah — by ship, by train and by covered wagon — from South Africa. He was three when his father died and his mother moved to Ophir — a mining camp Haywood recalled as one of the wildest in the West. He went to school in a little lumber shack, searched the dumps of nearby mines for iron pyrites and quartz crystals, fought boyhood wars with his classmates. He was often an eyewitness to violence — a Western-style street duel or the vigilance committee driving some culprit out of town. Here, as Haywood told it, he lost an eye when his knife slipped while making a slingshot. He left school when he was ten.

His first "strike" came a year later while living on a farm, working for his keep and a dollar a month. He had paused while driving a team of oxen to examine a nest of field mice. He suddenly felt the sting of a whiplash across his back. Without saying a word, he went to the farmhouse, collected his few possessions and walked ten miles to his home. When the farmer promised he would not repeat the whipping, Bill returned and worked out his time. He worked at odd jobs; then, when he was fifteen, went to Humboldt County, Nevada, where his step-father was superintendent of a mine.

His first job in the mine was wheeling rock. He remembered that he lightened his load each trip; "I was glad when quitting time came." Eagle Canyon was miles from nowhere in the Nevada desert. At night, the men

Labor History Archives, Wayne State University

WILLIAM D. HAYWOOD

talked or read, borrowing each other's books. Occasionally they traveled thirty miles or more to meet their distant neighbors and dance to a cigar-box tambourine and a three-stringed fiddle. At Eagle Canyon, too, from a tall, rawboned, chin-whiskered miner, Haywood first heard of the Knights of Labor. He read in the newspapers of the Haymarket bomb. He never forgot the last words of August Spies, who was hanged for his alleged part in the explosion: "There will come a time when our silence will be more powerful than the voices you are strangling today." To Haywood, "it was a turning point in my life."

He married his boyhood sweetheart, attempted to homestead a piece of Nevada land — only to lose it when it was made part of an Indian reservation. He remembered being impressed when militiamen, called out in the Pullman strike of 1894, jabbed their bayonets in the ground rather than fire on strikers. And he was impressed by the strike: "The big thing was that they could stop the trains." Soon he moved his family to Silver City, Idaho, and went to work in the Blaine mine.

Ed Boyce came to town in the fall of 1896 to sign up the hard-rock miners in the Western Federation of Miners. Haywood was shocked by Boyce's recollections of the Coeur d'Alene strike. A mill had been blown to bits when miners slid boxes of dynamite down a water flume. More than a thousand miners had been arrested and held in a bullpen by federal troops. Haywood was intrigued, too, by Boyce's account of the beginnings of the miners' union in Ada County jail in Boise. Haywood was one of the first to join, became an active union member who seldom missed a meeting. The local elected him president in 1898 and sent him to the union's 1898 convention.

The convention drew plans, Haywood recalled, to

strengthen the union's position "and back up the rifles that many of us already possessed." It also refused to listen to Sam Gompers, who had come to the convention in an effort to persuade the miners to join the AFL. Haywood remembered him as ". . . short and chunky . . . small, snapping eyes, a hard cruel mouth . . . a personality vain, conceited, petulant, and vindictive."

The miners went on strike again in 1899 in Coeur d'Alene, this time against a cut in pay. That cut meant, Haywood wrote, "less food, less clothes, less house-room, less schooling for the children, less amusements, less everything that made life worth living." An explosion ripped apart the Bunker Hill and Sullivan mill. Governor Frank Steunenberg, with the help of federal troops, put the district under martial law. Hundreds of miners were arrested, held for months without charges, many in a bullpen "unfit to house cattle." Haywood visited the district, saw the men behind the high, barbed-wire fence. "They were fighting my fight," he thought. "If their wages had been cut, my wages would have been cut. . . . Their appeals to the corporation went unheard. A mill had been blown up. If it was for this that they were in the bull-pen I should be there with them." One day soon after, while working in a tunnel, Haywood picked up an empty box and, on its side, wrote an angry resolution condemning Governor Steunenberg's actions. It was later published in the *Miners' Magazine*. A year later, for the last time, Haywood turned off the air on the machine drill he was using in a cross-cut three thousand feet below ground. He left that morning for the WFM convention at Denver. There he was elected secretary-treasurer of the union.

The war in the mines soon broke out with renewed ferocity. Union men and strikebreakers fought a pitched

battle at the Smuggler-Union in the San Juan district in
Colorado. Smeltermen chose July 4, 1903, to launch their
strike for an eight-hour day. The millmen in Telluride
walked out. Governor Peabody ordered in the militia and
thirty-three miners were forcibly deported. A reduction
plant in Colorado City fired forty-one union men. Again,
the militia took over. A compressor was blown up at Idaho
Springs, and union officials were driven from town by a
"Citizens' Protective League." Troops moved in at Cripple
Creek and the now-familiar bullpen reappeared. An explosion at the Vindicator mine killed the superintendent
and a foreman. When the Western Federation of Miners
met in convention in 1904, the delegates were stunned to
hear of an explosion at the Independence depot at Cripple
Creek that killed dozens and injured many more. Armed
scabs and deputies wrecked the union hall. Union relief
stores were smashed, tons of goods carried away. The
Victor *Record* was wrecked. General Sherman Bell ordered
strikers arrested and deported as vagrants. He replied to
protests: "What steps I take as military commander concern nobody but myself and my commander-in-chief. . . .
I don't want these men in Colorado."

The WFM convention that year called for a general
organization of labor that would embrace all workers in
one great union. That led to a secret meeting in Chicago
in January, 1905, where some thirty prominent socialists
(including Debs), radicals, labor leaders drafted a manifesto calling for "one great industrial union embracing all
industries." It would be founded on the class struggle; it
would reject any suggestion that the "irrepressible conflict
between the capitalist class and the working class" could
be reconciled. New machines are wiping out craft lines,
the manifesto declared. Ownership is becoming more con-

centrated. Craft unions offer no hope. It called for an organizational meeting in Chicago on June 27, 1905.

On that morning, in Brand's Hall, Haywood picked up a convenient piece of board and pounded on a table. "Fellow workers," he cried, "this is the Continental Congress of the working class. We are here to confederate the workers of this country into a working-class movement . . . to put the working class in possession of an economic power, the means of life, in control of the machinery of production and distribution, without regard to capitalist masters." Around him on the platform and in the audience were Gene Debs, leader of the Socialist Party and a vigorous advocate of industrial unionism; Mother Jones, an energetic union organizer despite her seventy-five years; Daniel De Leon, leader of the Socialist Trades and Labor Alliance; Lucy Parsons, widow of one of the anarchists hanged in the aftermath of the Haymarket explosion; Father Thomas J. Hagerty, a black-bearded man who insisted he was still a priest but without affiliation to his church. Among the nearly two hundred delegates, the Western Federation of Miners was the dominant organization. The motley collection was united in its opposition to the capitalist society and to craft unions, but the radicals differed, often sharply, on how these matters were to be corrected. For ten days they debated, then finally adopted a constitution. It began: "The working class and the employing class have nothing in common. There can be no peace as long as hunger and want are found among millions of working people and the few who make up the employing class have all the good things of life." The new organization's slogan was a modified version of the Knights' old motto: "An injury to one is an injury to all." It adopted the first of May as the holiday of the

98

American working class. Most of all, it called for revolutionary industrial unions — "by organizing industrially we
are forming the structure of the new society within the
shell of the old." It was named the Industrial Workers
of the World.

On December 30, 1905, former Governor Frank Steunenberg opened the gate to his home in Caldwell, Idaho,
triggering a homemade bomb that blew him to bits. This
was the same Steunenberg who had fought the miners in
1899 with militia and martial law and bullpen. The news,
Haywood commented, was "startling." A few weeks later,
Haywood was arrested at his roominghouse in Denver.
Charles Moyer, president of the WFM, was picked up as
he was about to leave to visit a union of smeltermen.
George Pettibone, a blacklisted miner turned small business-
man, was arrested at his home. The three were put on a
special train, taken at top speed — pausing only for coal
and water and then only at small stations — to Boise, Idaho.
There, they were jailed in "death row" in the Idaho peni-
tentiary, charged with murdering Frank Steunenberg. The
formalities of warrants and extradition were ignored. They
were kidnapped, Haywood declared, "in the dead of night."
The arrest and kidnapping provoked an angry outcry.
Appeal to Reason published a special edition, flaunting
Debs's provocative editorial: "Arise Ye Slaves. Their only
crime is loyalty to the working class." Miners organized a
defense fund and thousands of dollars poured in. The IWW
turned its newly organized energies to mobilizing support.
The U. S. Supreme Court refused to intervene in the
arrest; it was no more than an individual kidnapping, the
court decided. A lone justice objected that it could never
have been accomplished without the power of the two
states. President Theodore Roosevelt linked a bribe-taking

capitalist with Moyer, Haywood and Debs as "undesirable citizens." Haywood replied from his cell that "a man in [Roosevelt's] position should be the last to judge us until the case was decided in court." Debs called the President a liar.

Harry Orchard — "neatly dressed . . . clean shaven . . . well set-up, bluff, with an apparently open manner," according to Haywood — was the chief witness for the prosecution. His story offered the only link — an uncorroborated link, as it turned out — between Haywood and the bomb. It was a blood-curdling recital of murders and attempted murders, bombs and explosions. He claimed, among his many murderous exploits, to have lighted a fuse in the explosion that destroyed the Bunker Hill and Sullivan mill. He said he was responsible for the Vindicator explosion, the Independence depot explosion, for numerous attempts on the lives of public officials. He described in detail how he placed the bomb that killed Steunenberg. Haywood, Moyer and Pettibone, he claimed, were the instigators of his crimes. Haywood admitted his bitterness against the former governor but denied any part in his death. William E. Borah — the special prosecutor who had only recently been elected to the U. S. Senate — made a lengthy speech to the jury; an associate took nine hours more. Clarence Darrow, defending Haywood, talked for eleven hours. The next morning the jury returned a verdict of not guilty. The prosecution had offered no proof in support of Orchard's incredible tale. In mining camps throughout the West, Haywood recalled, tons of dynamite were exploded and he could not guess how much whiskey was drunk in the celebration that followed. Haywood turned down offers of thousands of dollars to appear in theaters and on the lecture platform. Instead he took to the road on behalf of the IWW, the Socialist Party, other working-class organizations and on behalf of Moyer and Pettibone (who, in due course, were also freed).

By 1908, the situation in the Western Federation of Miners was sharply changed. In the absence of Haywood and Moyer, a conservative leadership had taken over. The union had withdrawn from the IWW. Haywood was fired as a WFM representative by a brief notice in the *Miners' Magazine*. New leaders of the Wobblies,* backed by the "overall brigade" and the "red-blooded working stiffs," pulled the IWW's political teeth. Henceforth, its only goal would be to take over industry through its industrial revolutionary unions. It would have nothing to do with voting or with political parties. It would sign no agreements with any employer. It would, a leader said, "use any and all tactics that will get the results with the least expenditure of time and energy." It soon became the organization of the bindlestiff — the wandering worker whose worldly belongings were rolled into his blanket or "bindle" — the harvest hand, the migratory lumberjack, the hobo. Carleton Parker called the IWW "the only social break [in the wandering rank and file's] search for work . . . its headquarters the only competitor of the saloon in which they are welcome." The red card of the Wobbly gave the wandering worker status. "Hobo jungles" became IWW barracks. The men brought an "unquenchable zeal," endless poetry and song, countless leaflets and pamphlets and newspapers to their strikes and free-speech fights.

* No one seems to know the origin of this name for members of the IWW. It has been suggested that it was pinned on them by Harrison Gray Otis, union-hating publisher of the Los Angeles *Times*; others suggested it was derived from the inability of some foreign accents to deal with "w." Whatever the source, the name has stuck tight.

Increasingly the Wobblies were pictured as "arch-fiends and the dregs of society"; increasingly, public authorities attempted to suppress them. One result was a series of dramatic free-speech fights that ranged from one end of the Pacific slope to the other, from Walla Walla to San Diego, Missoula to Fresno. When city officials attempted to clamp down on their right to speak freely, to hold meetings, or distribute their endless literature, every footloose Wobbly — and that was most of them — moved into town, on foot or by the first available freight car. They crowded the forbidden street corners or parks, virtually demanding to be arrested. As one historian put it, they "almost literally broke into the jails." They jam-packed the jails, endured bullpens too crowded to let them lie down, were often met with unabashed violence and hostility. When they were forcibly deported, as they frequently were, they grabbed the next freight train back. Historian Paul F. Brissenden, in his history of the IWW, counted at least twenty important free-speech fights, lasting from a few days to months, between 1909 and 1913.

The Wobblies, too, led a series of valiant strikes, dramatic and often successful rebellions of the poor and the unskilled. At McKees Rock, Pennsylvania, the IWW organized a strike against the Pressed Steel Car Company. When a striker was killed by the state's notorious mounted police, the "Black Cossacks," the strikers sent word that they would kill three "cossacks" for every dead striker. A trooper was waylaid and killed; the police made no further use of their guns. "It was the only strike of the lower paid workers," Haywood claimed, "that has ever been won against the steel trust."

Under IWW leaders, some 25,000 textile workers at

Lawrence, Massachusetts, fought a bitter, two-and-a-half-month strike. In January, 1912, the woolen mills cut already meager wages when a state law enforced a reduction in hours. Wages ranging from $5.10 to $8.76 for a fifty-six-hour week were cut 20 to 30 cents when the work-week was reduced to fifty-four hours. The workers walked out. "It is the first strike I ever saw which sang," wrote Ray Stannard Baker, a well-known reporter of the time; "not only at the meetings did [the strikers] sing, but in the soup houses and in the streets. . . . They have a whole book of songs fitted to familiar tunes." The IWW organizers — Joseph Ettor and Arturo Giovanitti — were arrested on charges of murdering a girl striker. (They were later freed when numerous witnesses swore they saw police fire the shot.) Big Bill, busy raising money for the strike, came back to Lawrence and took over direction of the walkout. Strikers sent their children to be cared for in friendly homes in other cities; crowds of weeping parents and frightened children at the railroad station attracted wide attention. Haywood took sixteen strikers to testify at congressional hearings on the dispute. One was Camella Teoli, not yet fifteen, whose scalp had been torn from her head when her hair caught in a mill machine. She earned $6.55, she told the committee, and paid ten cents every two weeks for water on the job. The strike was met with militia and martial law; violence on the picket line was frequent, and it scarcely halted even when women strikers took over the picketing. After two and a half months, American Woolen Company granted wage increases of 5 to 20 per cent. Tens of thousands of textile workers throughout New England also won higher pay. With victory, however, the IWW lost interest. It had long maintained it would sign no agreements with employers; it was interested chiefly in stimulating protest and encouraging discontent. As a result, where it had claimed 13,000 members in Lawrence in January, 1912, it could only point to 700 in October, 1913.

In Paterson, New Jersey, the next year, a strike of workers in the silk mills and dye houses was met with a brave display of flags — on factories and stores, on "patriots'" lapels. A parade of strikers carried a sign:

We weave the flag.
We live under the flag.
We die under the flag.
But damn'd if we'll starve under the flag.

John Reed, a bright young Harvard-educated dramatic editor of *American Magazine* and a rising reporter, came to Paterson. He was arrested and jailed and freed only after New York newspapers headlined his predicament. He joined Haywood and others in staging at Madison Square Garden a dramatic pageant that stunned the city. In brief, colorful scenes, it told the story of the strike, the death of a picket, of a graveside service. It showed the strikers' children leaving their families to stay with sympathizers in other cities. In a final scene, hundreds of strikers streamed down the aisle to take part in a "typical" strike meeting. It was a propaganda success, and some thought it a dramatic success; but it was a financial flop. Its failure undermined the strikers' hopes. Soon they returned to work under much the same conditions they had left five months before.

Haywood was general organizer of the IWW, then general secretary. The national executive committee of the Socialist Party expelled him, in keeping with a resolution banning any member "who opposes political action or ad-

vocates crime, sabotage or other methods of violence." More
and more, the IWW opposed political action; it constantly
urged sabotage and direct action. It focused increasingly
on fanning "the flame of discontent," cared little for building stable, continuing unions.

"When the war broke out," Haywood wrote, "I was
struck dumb. For weeks I could scarcely talk." But he
was not speechless long. The IWW fought against the war
with typical energy. It refused to let any demands of
patriotism, real or imaginary, halt its efforts to organize
the most oppressed of the nation's workers. It led strikes
of loggers against filthy camps and rotten food and the
ten-hour day. Even the government could not persuade
some employers to establish the eight-hour day. In Arizona,
when copper miners struck for higher pay, more than a
thousand were rounded up, herded into cattle cars and
carried deep into the desert. For thirty-six hours they were
held without food or water. They were then put into a
stockade under army guard until the detention camp was
disbanded two months later. (Twenty-one leaders of the
Loyalty League that had rounded up the strikers were indicted. None was ever convicted.)

One Wobbly told Carleton Parker:
You ask me why the I.W.W. is not patriotic. . . .
If you were a bum without a blanket; if you had
left your wife and kids when you went West for a
job and had never located them since; if your job
never kept you long enough in one place to qualify
you to vote; if you slept in a lousy sour bunkhouse
and ate food just as rotten as they could give it to
you and get by with it . . . if every person who
represented law and order and the nation beat you

up, railroaded you to jail, and the good Christian
people cheered and told them to go to it, how the
hell do you expect a man to be patriotic?

The Wobblies were pictured, Brissenden writes, as "a
motley horde of hoboes and unskilled laborers who will
not work and whose philosophy is a philosophy simply of
sabotage and the violent overthrow of 'capitalism' . . . [as]
arch fiends and the dregs of society. It is the hang-them-all-
at-sunrise attitude." During the war, Brissenden says, most
IWW activities were "ordinary" strike activities, though
often met with "the night-stick and neck-tie party policy,"
and endless charges of disloyalty. Gene Debs, though he
had long since left its ranks, declared the IWW had "never
committed as much violence against the ruling class as
the ruling class has committed against the people."

More and more, the IWW came under special wartime
surveillance. Its meetings and activities were under constant watch. It was accused of receiving German money
and of obstructing the war. In September, 1917, at IWW
headquarters and offices across the country, Department
of Justice agents seized tons of books and records. In sub-
sequent raids, thousands of officers and members were
arrested and jailed. Haywood was arrested in the Chicago
raids. The following spring he went to trial before Judge
Kenesaw Mountain Landis, later baseball's famous "czar."
Government lawyers charged the IWW with sabotage and
conspiracy to obstruct the war. They poured records,
letters, editorials, pamphlets into the record, seeking to
prove that the IWW aimed to overthrow the government,
that it opposed the war and the draft, that it incited
sabotage and violence. Haywood's defense contended the
IWW sought to replace capitalist exploitation with a more
just society. Haywood took the stand and talked for days

about his experiences in the mines, his knowledge of misery among the lowly. He said the IWW had never obstructed the war, though it never supported it. He admitted he favored sabotage: "the biggest, strongest and most wholesome weapon of the working class." Haywood was found guilty, as were scores of others. He was sentenced to a total of thirty-eight years in prison and $30,000 in fines. The U. S. Court of Appeals refused to intervene and steps were taken to carry his appeal to the Supreme Court. Haywood, though, was increasingly fascinated by the Russian Revolution. He had little hope of a favorable decision from the Supreme Court; his health was poor. "My friends thought it would be an unnecessary sacrifice for me to spend the rest of my life in prison." He left the country, abandoning the bond that had been posted for him. He traveled to Riga, then to Moscow. He hoped to find what he had once said would be "the IWW all feathered out." He died of a stroke in Moscow on May 18, 1928. His ashes were buried half in the Kremlin Wall, the other half, at his request, in Waldheim Cemetery in Chicago, close by the graves of the Haymarket anarchists.

The Wobblies, Brissenden concludes, raised questions about the organization of the unskilled, about the relative merits of craft unionism and industrial unionism, the quality of democracy in industrial life. The IWW, he says, was "grotesquely unprepared for responsibility"; it had posed its questions "crudely." They were answered with the full weight of the law. The raids of 1917 and the trials of 1918, for most purposes, wiped out the IWW. It held a convention in Chicago in 1955 — fifty years to the day from the time of its launching. It was attended by eight delegates and five officers. Our membership, the general secretary said, is at a "low ebb."

CHAPTER SEVEN

William Green

"Labor is safe . . ."

"THE BUSINESS of America," declared President Calvin Coolidge, "is business." It was: never more than in the 1920s. The attitudes of business colored the society of the day — a time of unfettered free enterprise, a rising stock market, the glow of easy money. It was a time, too, of the open shop, loudly and defiantly proclaimed. Employers smashed unions, broke strikes, vigorously stamped out the seed of unionism wherever it dropped.

Union membership climbed over the five million mark in 1920. Four years later, more than a million and a half workers had left the unions. A short, sharp depression forced them out, then an intensive, widespread open-shop drive. For the next half-dozen years the ranks held steady, then fell further as the depression bit into them. One of every eight workers in the nation's work force belonged to a union in 1920; one in fourteen a decade later.

The Mine Workers under John L. Lewis lost tens of thousands of members. The Ladies Garment Workers, torn by a bitter internal fight, shrunk to a third of its size.

The International Seamen's Union was driven off most of the nation's ships; the members, a historian noted, "melted away, vanished, disappeared." Prohibition drove thousands of workers from the Hotel and Restaurant Employees and the brewery workers' unions. Still, the skilled crafts hung on and, in a few cases, actually increased their membership.

Farmers abandoned their land for jobs in the city, bringing their antiunion tradition with them. Immigrants seeking a new life found little in unions to attract them; many without skills were excluded. Expanding industries, such as autos, chemicals, rubber, kept the unions out; others, like textiles, moved into the nonunion South. The courts upheld the "yellow dog" contract that could require a man, to get a job or hold one, to swear he would never join a union. The courts also nullified laws prohibiting child labor and fixing minimum wages for women and children. The experts said a family needed close to $2,000 a year to live in "health and decency." The average industrial worker never earned as much as $1,500. By the end of the decade, thousands of steelworkers still worked seven days, eighty-four hours a week; women and children worked fifty-four to seventy hours a week in textile mills. In 1928, a visiting Australian unionist observed: "Labour organization exists only by tolerance of employers. . . . It has no real part in determining conditions." Magazine articles proclaimed the failure, the collapse, the twilight of the union movement.

Ill, tired, hemmed in by friend and foe and habit, the aged Sam Gompers did nothing to stem the tide. On December 13, 1924, he died. Matthew Woll, the short, dapper chief of the Photo Engravers, was regarded by many as the "crown prince." The veteran James Duncan,

Merkle Press

WILLIAM GREEN

first vice-president, hoped he could close out his career by serving as president until the next convention. John L. Lewis, president of the powerful United Mine Workers, who had run against Gompers in 1921, also eyed the throne. If he could not have it, he at least would have a decisive hand in choosing the man who would. The executive council settled on William Green, third vice-president of the Federation and secretary-treasurer of the Mine Workers. "Labor is safe under Green's leadership," a Richmond newspaper commented. "Capital has nothing to fear during his regime, and the public is fortunate in having him as the responsible spokesman of a highly important group of citizens."

This "plain . . . plodding . . . undramatic" man was the son of a Welsh miner who had come with his wife to Coshocton, Ohio, in 1870. There, in a miner's shack on Hardscrabble Hill, their son William was born on March 3, 1873. William was educated briefly in a one-room school. He earned his first money — a five-dollar gold piece — reading the Bible to his illiterate father, "a silent little man with long white hair and beard," who kept his family on the $1.50 a day he earned in the mine. The family had a few turkeys and hogs and a cow; it had enough to eat and little more. William carried water for a railroad gang when he was fourteen. The next year he went to work in the Morgan Run mine. He came to know the danger of gas and the sound of the cave-in, and he helped to carry home the crushed bodies of its victims. And he joined the union.

He was elected secretary of the union when he was eighteen, later treasurer, then president. In 1900, he was made president of the subdistrict; six years later, of the Ohio district. He left the mine in 1908 to devote full time to union work. "As a union official," he recalled, "I was continually emphasizing the significance of collective bargaining and how much further we could get by using our heads than by using our fists." He married when he was twenty-one, became the father of five daughters and a son. He was a member of the Elks, the Odd Fellows, the Masons and the Democratic Party.

Bill Green was elected to the Ohio Senate in 1911 and served two terms. He sponsored the law that established "run of the mine" coal as the basis of miners' pay. Until then, miners had been paid only for coal over a specified size. He authored the state's workmen's compensation act. In 1911, he was appointed statistician of the Mine Workers, two years later became its secretary-treasurer. In that year — 1913 — the seventh vice-presidency of the AFL fell vacant. It was offered to Miners' President John P. White, but he rejected it as beneath his dignity. Instead, it went to his second in command, William Green. By the time Lewis engineered Green's selection as the successor to Gompers, he had risen, merely by the passage of time, to the third vice-president's chair.

Bill Green was a round-faced, bland-looking man, well and conservatively dressed. He was a religious man — the Green family had held daily religious observances, and at one time he had aspired to the ministry. His sponsor was to comment bitterly — and unfairly — some years later: "Bill and I had offices next door to each other for ten years. . . . I have done a lot of exploring in Bill's mind and I give you my word there is nothing there." Green was more the conciliator in the Federation than the leader. He won the support of the powerful union leaders on the executive council — Dan Tobin of the Teamsters, Bill Hutcheson and Frank Duffy of the Carpenters, Matthew Woll. He also saw the power shift — from the presidency, where Gompers had held it, to the executive council. Green became the balance wheel and spokesman for its majority.

Green shouldered Gompers' policies with little difficulty. He differed, though, on one crucial point. As a miner, he believed in industrial unions — that was the tradition of the miners. He did not press the point, however. As the new head of the AFL, he held out a friendly hand to employers. Hostility, he reminded them, inevitably created the tactics of force; labor preferred the conference table. He told the employers they needed the mass markets that only high wages could offer. He claimed workers were entitled in justice to increased wages that reflected their rising productivity. He lectured at Harvard, to service clubs, wherever he could get an audience. His voice went unheard.

In 1925, Green argued that labor's interest lay in making production more efficient, in harmony rather than conflict. He preached — in a few instances, participated in — union-management arrangements aimed at improving efficiency. The bulk of industry was not interested. In 1927, the AFL authorized an organizing drive among auto workers that never really got started. In 1929, Green toured the mill towns of the South. Rising industry in the South offered the labor movement in the late twenties an inviting opportunity — tens of thousands of unorganized, poorly paid, exploited workers. Green preached unionism and higher living standards as the way to build bigger markets — and profits — and as the way to defend the nation against the threat of communism. Always he underscored the absence of any common ground between the AFL and any kind of radicalism. Nor did unionism challenge the racially segregated economy of the South. For years, segregation

113

had been the labor movement's response to the growing industrial role of the Negro.

In 1927, the Federation began publishing statistics on unemployment among its members. Its measure was crude and inadequate, but in February, 1928, it noted an ominous rise in joblessness among organized workers. It saw the rise as a danger sign since "skilled workers . . . generally are not among the first laid off." In May, 1929, the AFL urged a national employment service and a census of unemployment. In November, after the Wall Street crash, President Hoover as well as William Green urged industry to avoid wage cuts and speed up investment in new plants and materials.

The AFL seemed stunned, almost paralyzed, by the reach and the speed of the depression that rolled over the nation. It had never supported any kind of social insurance, other than workmen's compensation. In 1932, with some fifteen million out of work, it urged the adoption of unemployment insurance. In the same year, it also urged the thirty-hour week as its answer to the depression. It called for more public works, for preference in jobs to those with dependents, for more generous relief from both private and public funds. Green warned the country that the workers could only be pushed so far "before they will turn on [their exploiters] and destroy them. . . . Revolutions grow out of the depths of hunger." Across the country, the unemployed began to organize; radical movements of every color became more active. The Federation's membership, which had dropped steadily since 1927, fell to only slightly more than two million in 1933. When Franklin Delano Roosevelt challenged Herbert Hoover in the 1932 presidential election, the AFL sat out the campaign — as it almost always had. President Green urged union mem-

114

bers to vote for "the advancement of human welfare and responsible government."

In the spring of 1933, President Roosevelt proposed — and Congress quickly enacted — the National Industrial Recovery Act. It authorized industry to draft codes of fair practices that would establish minimum wages and maximum hours of work and ease antitrust restrictions on production and pricing policies. Most important of all, the act set forth Section 7(a) — the now famous guarantee of the right of workers to organize in unions of their own choosing and to bargain collectively without interference or coercion.

With Section 7(a) at his back, John L. Lewis invested the last penny in the Mine Workers' treasury in a sweeping organizing drive. In four months, he tripled the size of his union, recaptured the South and Middle West — areas that had been lost during the past ten years. The Ladies Garment Workers mounted an intensive drive; twelve thousand workers joined from New York alone. Across the country, in response to the new charter of freedom they saw in Section 7 (a), workers poured into old unions or organized new ones in industry after industry. Dormant unions came to life. Charter applications poured in from rubber workers and steel fabricators and auto mechanics, from West Virginia shoe workers, Ohio boilermakers, Detroit auto workers and California clerks. By August, 1934, in barely a year, the AFL gained some 700,000 new members. In 1933, three times as many workers went out on strike as in 1932. In 1934, the Pacific Coast longshoremen and maritime workers, the Kohler workers, the textile workers, the Minneapolis teamsters were among many who fought to establish their right (already proclaimed in law) to organize and bargain collectively. For many employers,

Arthur Schlesinger, Jr. observes, conceding that right "meant, they believed, irretrievable disaster. Each side felt it was fighting for its life. The result in some communities approached civil war."

Against that clamorous backdrop, the American Federation of Labor met in 1934 in San Francisco. A sharp, sometimes bitter internal dispute erupted. New unions in the mass-production industries — auto, steel, aluminum and such — cried for industrial union charters. They wanted the right to organize their plants from top to bottom, taking in every worker from the least to the most skilled; craftsmen as well as production-line workers, common laborers and highly skilled journeymen. They pointed to the familiar industrial-union pattern of the mine workers and brewery workers. Thousands upon countless thousands could be organized, they said, in new industrial unions. But the powerful craft unions were reluctant to move. For years, sometimes a half-century and more, they had organized members of their particular craft wherever they worked. They had ignored workers of lesser or of different skills, concentrating only on their special craft and its related workers. They had used their members' high skills to devise elaborate systems of apprenticeship and working rules to control the entrance of new workers into their craft. Now they foresaw industrial unions breaking down their prized craft lines, sweeping up their craftsmen and burying them in a mass of unskilled and semiskilled industrial workers. After years of fighting endless border wars to safeguard their craft lines, they were not about to yield even an inch to these insistent newcomers. Leading the craft unionists into battle were Hutcheson of the Carpenters, John P. Frey of the Metal Trades and Dan Tobin of the Teamsters, who made it plain that he saw no place in

116

the labor movement for "the rubbish that have lately come
into other organizations." Industrial-union supporters, John
L. Lewis at their head, insisted that craft unions were
incapable of organizing mass production industry. The
craft unions, solid, conservative, thoroughly seasoned, stood
pat. Finally, after six days of patient negotiations, Lewis
and Vice-President Matthew Woll arrived at a compromise
agreement. The executive council was directed to issue
charters for national unions in auto, cement, aluminum
and such other mass production industries as might be
necessary. The Federation was instructed to launch an
immediate organizing campaign in steel. Provisionally, the
new unions would be controlled by the executive council
to safeguard the jurisdiction of existing unions.

When the Federation met in Atlantic City the following
year, the debate was promptly and bitterly resumed. The
industrial-union forces charged the executive council with
utter failure; after fifty-five years, they pointed out, only
10 per cent of the nation's workers had been enlisted in
the union cause. Its policies were unfitted to the needs
of workers in mass production industries. They did not
intend, the industrial-union spokesmen insisted, to drain
off the members of craft unions into great industrial organizations. They intended simply to organize the unorganized
workers in mass production industries. These could be
effectively organized only on industrial, plant-wide lines
without regard to jurisdiction. Lewis took the floor. The
AFL could no longer afford to ignore the cry of the unorganized, he warned. "Heed this cry from the hearts of
men. . . ." he pleaded. "Organize the unorganized and in
doing this make the American Federation of Labor the
greatest instrument that has ever been forged to befriend
the cause of humanity and champion human rights." His
appeal went unheeded; the convention voted down the

industrial-union proposal. Soon after, Big Bill Hutcheson of the Carpenters raised a point of order against an industrial-union delegate seeking to state his union's case. Lewis exchanged a few blunt, angry words with Hutcheson, then strode across the aisle and knocked him sprawling with one wild haymaker. That dramatic, probably deliberate, blow symbolized the decisive split in the house of labor.

CHAPTER EIGHT

John L. Lewis

"Think of me
as a coal miner . . ."

JOHN L. LEWIS stood six feet tall that day in Atlantic
City when he poked Big Bill Hutcheson in the nose.
He carried about two hundred and ten pounds on a
thick, bulky frame, topped by great, shaggy eyebrows
and a long, loose mane of hair. He was given to quoting
Shakespeare or the Bible in a deep, powerful voice, lard-
ing his speeches with generous splashes of insult and
epithet, with anger or pleading, with fact or his own brand
of fancy. His library held many a volume on Lincoln and
Napoleon, economics and the classics. It also held, a reporter noted, "a morass of detective stories." In the hallway
of his home, he kept a miner's pick.

John L. Lewis was a puzzle — and became even more
of one. To a colleague, late one afternoon, Lewis wondered:
"What makes me tick? Is it power I'm after, or am I a
Saint Francis in disguise, or what?" His utterances, wrote
Arthur Schlesinger, Jr., "gave the sorrows and aspirations
of all labor a new dignity. Across the country, people
recognized in him — some with hope, some with fear — the
authentic voice of a great social force." Lewis proclaimed:

"Let the workers organize. Let the toilers assemble. Let their crystallized voice proclaim their injustices and demand their privileges. Let all thoughtful citizens sustain them, for the future of labor is the future of America." He later led a series of bitter wartime strikes in the nation's vital coal mines. To *Fortune,* at the time, he was the nation's outstanding "bad-man symbol." Nearly three-quarters of the ballots in one of its polls voted him the country's "most harmful individual." Overseas, soldiers swore at his name. He was deplored and excused, damned and praised, cussed and endlessly discussed.

"The thing that gives me strength," Lewis once told the miners, "is the fact that I am able correctly to interpret the aims of my people. I know the psychology of the coal miner . . . his dreams and his ideals and trials and tribulations. I have lived with coal miners. I am one of them." His own opinions were worth little, Lewis went on. "It is only when I am able to translate your dreams and aspirations into words . . . that my tongue possesses any strength or my hand has any force." And then he has spoken — "not in the quavering tones of a feeble mendicant asking alms, but in the thundering voice of the captain of a mighty host, demanding the rights to which men are entitled."

"Think of me as a coal miner," he once said, "and you won't make any mistake." Miners were something of a people apart. They lived in shabby little mining camps, cut off from the rest of the world. They spent their lives in company houses and in debt to the company store. They worked deep beneath the ground with danger and death always at their side. "The price of coal, always cheap," said Saul Alinsky, "was for years higher than the

120

United Mine Workers of America

JOHN L. LEWIS

price of human life." Their common and miserable existence forged a binding link among them.

His family, Lewis noted, had "been associated with the mining industry for a century and a half." His father, a coal miner, left Wales when his union collapsed. He settled after a time in Lucas, Iowa, where he dug coal for the White Breast Fuel Company. On Lincoln's Birthday, in 1880, in the tiny town of Lucas, his first son was born and was named John Llewellyn. The boy could little more than toddle when Tom led a strike of the Knights of Labor at White Breast. He was blacklisted. For years he wandered the state, dragging his growing family with him. He worked where he could — until the blacklist caught up with him and forced him to move on. Fifteen years later, the blacklist was lifted, and he returned to Lucas.

John had pieced together something of an education during his family's wanderings, but he quit school when the family returned to Lucas. "I got along all right in school," he recalled, "but I was just interested in outside things." He went to work in the mines, ten and twelve hours a day. Still, he found time to play shortstop on a baseball team and manage a debating team. For a while, he quit digging and tried running a mill, working as a carpenter, even managing the local opera house. When he was twenty-one, he took to the road. He dug copper and silver and coal in Rocky Mountain mines. He helped to carry out the bodies of 169 miners who died in a fire in a Wyoming pit. He returned to Lucas half a dozen years later and married the daughter of the local doctor. Myrta Edith Bell, a biographer notes, was to give Lewis "love, nurture his delicate ego, discipline his reading and thinking, and improve his platform style." She gave him two daughters, one of whom died young, and a son.

122

In 1909, John moved his family to Panama, Illinois, followed shortly by his five brothers. Back in Lucas, some people said, "Those Lewises; if you lick one of 'em you have to lick 'em all." With their help, John was elected president of the miners' union. In 1911, he went to Springfield as the miners' legislative representative. His work caught Sam Gompers' eye, and Sam put him to work for the AFL. He organized workers in a score or more of industries; he spoke for labor in state and national capitals. Lewis learned, *Fortune* magazine once commented, "the soundness of Gompers's doctrine that tactics, not ideals, make a labor movement." In the United Mine Workers, Lewis served on the interstate wage negotiating committee, presided over the annual convention as acting chairman, served as its chief statistician, and vice-president. The president, Frank Hayes, was out of action much of the time from illness or drink. Lewis took over in his place. In 1921, he formally became president of the United Mine Workers of America.

Lewis took over the president's job when the union was near the peak of its strength, but when the coal industry was sick unto death. The capacity of the mines had been stretched by the heavy demands and high prices of the war — stretched far beyond the needs of the country at peace. Oil, gas, electric power faced coal with tough, relentless competition. Coal prices dropped, and operators attempted to meet the problem by cutting costs. When they could not force union wages down, they mechanized or they opened up nonunion mines with cheap nonunion labor. The nation's coal-producing capacity — 60 per cent more than the country was using at the end of the war — climbed to twice the nation's needs. The union won a 27 per cent wage increase in 1920, fought a bitter strike in

1922 to hold on to it. The union made its point, but when it returned to work it left stranded some hundred thousand nonunion miners who had come out at the union's strike call. Still more miners left the union as operators turned on the pressure to cut costs still further. Union mines were closed, then reopened under nonunion conditions. Some operators closed their union mines in the North and opened nonunion pits in the Southern fields. Lewis won a renewal of their agreement in 1924 — the so-called Jacksonville agreement — until 1927. But the union lost still more members, still more mines. Lewis cried, "No backward step," but the membership continued to dwindle. Aided by company towns and company police, by company-dominated courts and newspapers, the operators — so Professor Irving Bernstein asserts — "set about the systematic destruction of the union."

Lewis fought off the operators with one hand; with the other, he cut down the opposition inside the union. When Alex Howat led his Kansas district on a series of strikes against a compulsory arbitration law, Lewis expelled him. Howat fought back through the union and in the court. He got his final answer in 1924 when he was thrown bodily off the platform at the miners' convention. Lewis struck down Frank Farrington, another potential rival. He produced evidence that Farrington, president of the Illinois district, had accepted a $25,000 fee to act as labor-relations adviser to a coal producer. Farrington's expulsion opened a new chain of events that ended in the early 1930s in the formation of a short-lived dual union, the Progressive Miners of America. John Brophy, head of District 2 in Pennsylvania, called for an organizing drive, nationalization of the mines, reinstatement for the expelled.

In 1926, he ran against Lewis for the presidency. In time, he, too, was driven from the union.

By 1928, Lewis could no longer hold the line. Nonunion competition pressed in from every direction. Each district was released to make the best deal it could. Pay reductions ran from a third in Ohio to 20 per cent in Illinois and Indiana. Nonunion miners were digging 85 per cent of the nation's coal. But Lewis was in full, unchallenged control of the union. He ran its conventions with a tight fist. "If there are any delegates who feel inclined to insult the chairman," he told one convention, "let them step up here on the platform and try it." To another delegate, he said bluntly, "take that gun out of your pocket or I'll shove it down your throat." By 1930, Lewis reigned over little more than a shell of a union. It had lost more than half its members and most of the major coal fields. "He killed more than the leaders of our union," one insurgent group of miners declared. "He killed its very soul." *Fortune* described him as "labor's most conspicuous flop." Both the industry and the union were totally demoralized.

In the immediate post-World War I years, Lewis had briefly advocated putting the mines under government ownership. But in 1925, he published a book urging the free play of economic forces in the coal industry. ("Would that mine enemy had written a book," he moaned years later.) The nation's mines became increasingly nonunion, standards fell and unemployment spread; Lewis looked for other means of rescuing the industry and his members' jobs. He proposed a bill to stabilize coal production, but Congress ignored it. As the depression deepened, more thought was given the idea of allowing producers to regulate production and control prices. In return, Lewis insisted on guarantees for the miners. In 1933, some of these ideas — self-regulation of production coupled with guarantees for labor — were reflected in the National Industrial Recovery Act. Especially important was Section 7(a), the declaration of labor's right to organize.

Lewis invested the UMW's treasury in organizers and turned them loose in the coal fields. "The President wants you to unionize," their leaflets shouted. "The law is on our side." By tens of thousands, miners returned to the union. Less than four months later, Lewis signed a new agreement with both Northern and Southern operators. Within a year the union's membership leaped from 150,000 to 515,000. The nation's coal industry once again was union — with the sole but important exception of the "captive" mines, those owned by the great steel firms. Opposition had been thoroughly drained from the union; Lewis' control was unquestioned. He had a solid foundation and generous resources to back him in what he now considered the big job: unionizing the nation's unorganized workers. The captive coal mines and the steelworkers headed his list. Later, Lewis explained why: the low pay of the unorganized steelworkers was a drag on better wages for the miners. Nor could the mine workers tolerate the competition of the lower wages of the miners working in the steel companies' mines. Until these wages were raised to "a human, decent standard," no miner could ever be sure of "a just wage." Lewis told a biographer, Saul Alinsky, "This seemed to be a simple elementary economic fact and it applied not only to the miners, but also to other organized union groups."

Years later, Lewis told of a midnight conversation with William Green soon after the passage of the NIRA. Lewis said he urged Green to launch an immediate organizing campaign, promising him the UMW's last dollar. "Now, John," Lewis said Green replied, "let's take it easy." That night, Lewis said, he knew the AFL would never do the job. His doubts were momentarily eased when the 1934 AFL convention ordered the executive council to issue a number of industrial-union charters. But the 1934 resolution was not implemented and the 1935 convention turned down the industrial-union forces' proposals. Lewis was disappointed, but not surprised. That summer, at a long Sunday breakfast, he had discussed a growing idea with a number of his close advisers. He discussed it again, this time with a handful of union leaders, on the last day of the convention, in the shadow of the defeat of the industrial-union program — and of Lewis' wild haymaker. On November 9, 1935, they met again in Washington, D. C. That day Lewis announced the formation of the Committee for Industrial Organization — almost immediately shortened to CIO. Its purpose, the announcement said, was to encourage and promote "the organization of the unorganized workers in mass production industries and other industries upon an industrial basis" and "to bring them under the banner and in affiliation with the American Federation of Labor." Lewis was chairman; Charles P. Howard, president of the Typographical Union but acting on his own, was secretary. Sidney Hillman of the Amalgamated Clothing Workers and David Dubinsky of the International Ladies Garment Workers Union had been members of the Atlantic City group. Now they were joined by Thomas F. McMahon of the United Textile Workers, Max Zaritsky of the Hatters, Harvey C. Fremming of the Oil Workers and Thomas H. Brown of the Mine, Mill and Smelter Workers. For director, Lewis designated John Brophy, one of the many insurgents who had once been expelled from the UMW by Lewis. He was one of a large number of former Lewis opponents in the UMW who went to work for him in the CIO.

Two weeks later, President Green sent each member of the CIO a warning: continuation of the committee could lead to "dual" unionism, to bitterness and strife; the unions, after all, were bound by the majority decision of the convention. He urged the committee to dissolve. Lewis angrily resigned as vice-president of the AFL. Secretary Howard replied, more calmly, that the CIO did not intend to "raid" the membership of any other union, invade the jurisdiction of any other union, or encourage any unionism "dual" to the AFL. Lewis added an almost personal message to Green. "It is bruited about . . . that your private sympathies and individual inclinations lie with the group espousing the industrial type of organization" — a reference to Green's long-standing leaning toward industrial unions — "while your official actions and public utterances will be in support of their adversaries. . . . Why not return to your father's house?" Lewis offered to step aside and make Green chairman in his place. Green replied indignantly that he was already in his "father's house." Big Bill Hutcheson of the Carpenters demanded immediate expulsion of the CIO unions. Arthur Wharton of the Machinists swore he "would rather see the labor movement go under and myself in hell than have John L. Lewis get away with it."

Pressure mounted in the executive council to suspend the CIO unions. Once more, it called on the CIO to dissolve. Lewis gave Green a dramatic answer at the miners' own convention: "All the members of the executive council of the American Federation of Labor will be wearing asbestos suits in hell before that committee is dissolved."

When the CIO unions refused to answer the charges laid against them by the executive council, they were suspended. Green, at one point, had questioned the power of the council to do it, but he changed his mind. George Harrison of the Railway Clerks still doubted that the council was acting within its authority. David Dubinsky, the lone CIO member on the council, voted against suspension. But it was done. The 1936 convention affirmed the suspension in the absence of the CIO unions. There was talk that the Mine Workers would retaliate by expelling Green. He replied that it would not affect his standing, since he carried an honorary gold card in the Musicians' Union. Lewis snorted: "That's appropriate. Like Nero, Green fiddles while Rome burns."

Steel was John L. Lewis' prime target. "As long as Big Steel is free to tack up a sign at a single pit-head announcing a wage cut," *Fortune* said, "the United Mine Workers are in danger of becoming, as they were once before, a mere rear-guard of labor's retreat to cooliedom." Big Steel's captive mines remained the sword over the miner's head. Through the first six months of 1936, both the AFL and CIO dangled offers of assistance before the tiny, impotent Amalgamated Association of Iron and Steel Workers. Its books in 1935 carried fewer than ten thousand members. It disbanded eighty-four lodges that year, organized only four. The AFL offered help without being too specific; it added that it would have to respect the "jurisdictional rights" of other international unions. Lewis promised $500,000, pledged he would keep the industrial-union basis of the organization, and insisted on low dues to encourage a mass sign up. The association was torn. It met with the executive council, then asked a meeting with Lewis. He replied: "Your executive board must decide whether it will cooperate or obstruct. If you do not yet know your own mind, please stay at home."

In June, the CIO reached an understanding with the Amalgamated and almost at once announced the formation of the Steel Workers' Organizing Committee. Lewis made Philip Murray, his longtime lieutenant in the UMW, its director. Organizers poured into the steel towns. *Fortune* reported, "Offices have been opened in towns that never saw a union office before. Signs have been carried in streets where no union ever before dared to raise its head. And practically every day meetings are held in that vast territory, openly or furtively, in parks, in convention halls, in cockeyed shacks on the edges of town, or even on isolated farms leased for the occasion."

The Iron and Steel Institute took its stand in 375 newspapers across the country. It denounced the "outsiders" running the union campaign. It pledged its loyalty to the open shop and its undying resistance to what it called "coercion and intimidation." It claimed to be devoted to the principle of collective bargaining and cited the existence throughout the industry of employee representation plans — the unionists insisted they were company-controlled. The steelmakers laid up huge stores of tear gas and riot guns and hired more labor spies. Still the workers flooded into the SWOC. Big company unions joined in bodies. By January, 1937, SWOC claimed 125,000 members.

Through the same hectic months of 1936, unionism spread into almost every sector of industry. Nearly 800,000 workers took part in work stoppages. Most of the strikes were fought simply for the right to organize a union. Countless thousands — auto workers, electrical workers, rubber workers, clothing workers and more — were on the move. "It is a good time," Lewis noted, "to hit your ad-

versary when he is looking in other fields." The impatient
auto workers gave him the chance.

In mid-December Lewis called on General Motors to
"do a little collective bargaining." William S. Knudsen,
head man at the big auto firm, granted the unionists what
he called a "personal interview." He told them that the
workers' complaints would have to be taken up by local
plant managers. The workers' response, in one GM plant
after another, was simply to sit down. The sitdown strike
was not a new tactic; other workers at other times had
sat down, stayed in, slowed down, walked off. The rubber
workers had used the sitdown successfully the winter before. Now the auto workers sat down. If it was not new,
it was surprising. Newspaper editorials and irate employers
denounced the sitdowns as illegal seizures, trespassing,
general insurrection. The strikers argued that the sitdown
was merely an orderly, effective — and peaceful — way of
striking. Lewis simply said, "feed them and tell them to
invite their friends." He put the CIO squarely behind
them.

General Motors refused to consider negotiations until the
workers left the plants; even then, national recognition was
out of the question. The auto workers shut down still more
plants. The company asked a court to order the strikers
to get out of the plant; Judge Edward Black at Flint
promptly complied. When the auto workers revealed that
the judge owned $219,000 worth of General Motors stock,
the judge was discredited, his order ignored. Encouraged
by the organization of an antiunion, strikebreaking force
called the Flint Alliance, police attempted to stop deliveries
of food to the sitdowners. A riot broke out. Governor
Murphy brought company and union representatives together and obtained an agreement: the strikers would leave

five major plants that weekend; General Motors would start talks Monday. Strikers began to leave the plants, flags flying and bands playing. Then the union learned that General Motors had agreed, at almost the same time, to negotiate with the Flint Alliance. Crying "double-cross," the auto workers promptly halted the evacuation.

The Auto Workers feared that the company would be able to reopen enough plants to get back into production; it prepared to spread the strike. Union leaders made elaborate preparations to call a strike in Chevrolet plant Number 9. The company, informed by its labor spies of the union's plans, concentrated guards and police on the plant. The union quickly moved four hundred men into Chevrolet Plant Number 4, a strategic plant that had been the union's secret target right along. Production now was completely crippled, coming to a virtual standstill.

A second court injunction ordered the men to leave the plants. The sheriff was directed to enforce it. The strikers barricaded the windows of the plants with sheets of steel and sent Governor Murphy a telegram: "We have no illusions about the sacrifices which this decision will entail. We fully expect that if a violent effort to oust us is made many of us will be killed, and we take this means of making it known to our wives, our children, to the people of the state of Michigan and the country that if this result follows from the attempt to eject us, you are the one who must be held responsible for our deaths."

John L. Lewis left New York for what he hoped would be peace negotiations in Detroit. Faced with a demand that he order the strikers out of the plants, Lewis refused. He added that he did not doubt the ability of the state to "shoot the members of our union out of those plants." But he wanted it known that, if the order were issued, "the militia will have the pleasure of shooting me out of the plants with them."

For eight days, Governor Murphy held Lewis and Knudsen in negotiations. At one point, William Green phoned Murphy, urging him not to settle the strike without considering the rights of the craft unions. Lewis exploded and reached for his hat. When the governor asked where he was going, Lewis told him to settle the strike with Green or Haile Selassie (former emperor of Ethiopia), who probably had as many members in the plants as Green.

At the start of the strike General Motors was turning out 53,000 cars; its production after six weeks was down to 110 units. Finally — early on the morning of Lewis' fifty-seventh birthday — General Motors yielded. It granted the auto workers exclusive bargaining rights for six months in some twenty plants where the union represented a majority of the workers. In other plants, the union retained the right to represent its members. The strikers would be returned to work without discrimination. Bill Knudsen said: "Let us have peace and make cars." *The New York Times* and *Time* suggested Lewis had fallen far short of his target. Lewis pointed out that seven weeks before, General Motors would not deal with or recognize a labor union — it never had and it had proclaimed it never would. Now the union has an "entirely satisfactory" contract that paves the way for "an adjusted relationship." Before, Lewis added, members had been fired for wearing union emblems. Now, they may wear their union buttons. The contract ended any "confusion" about that. The auto workers pushed ahead. In following months, other strikes at other companies consolidated the union's position. Only Ford remained and, eventually, Ford signed too.

Meantime, the steel situation was coming to a quiet

boil. Early in January, shortly before Lewis went to Detroit, he encountered Myron C. Taylor, chairman of the board of United States Steel, in the dining room of a Washington hotel. Lewis suggested the two might get together. Taylor agreed, and they set a meeting for the next day. That was the first of a series of meetings that continued up to, and then resumed after, the auto settlement. Taylor was aware of the uprising of the steelworkers, of the movement of company unions into the Steel Workers' Organizing Committee. He must have suspected, too, the pressures that would flow from Washington and the White House if Big Steel and labor came to blows. At the time, too, the British were shopping in the U. S. for sources of steel. Added to which, *Fortune* suggested, Taylor did not wholly agree with the last-ditch, all-out, open-shop attitude of the steel bosses. Whatever Taylor's reasons, business, government and labor were stunned when, on March 1, 1937, U. S. Steel recognized the SWOC. Phil Murray, head of the Steel Workers, and Benjamin Fairless, head of Carnegie-Illinois, the principal U. S. Steel subsidiary, signed a collective bargaining agreement. Ironically, it was concluded under a picture of the dour Andrew Carnegie, founder of the company. It was to the vacationing Carnegie in 1892 that Henry Clay Frick had reported the company's victory over the Homestead steel strikers: "Do not think we will ever have any serious labor trouble again. . . . We had to teach our employees a lesson and we have taught them one that they will never forget." Carnegie replied: "Life worth living again . . . congratulate all around."

Coming on the heels of the auto settlement, the Lewis-Taylor agreement was a major landmark for American unionism. Taken together, they represented critical and de-

cisive victories over two of the largest and most important
— probably the most important — strongholds of the antiunion open shop. They gave unionism a sturdy foothold
in two giant basic industries. They gave fresh impetus to
the CIO drive in countless others.

But the war continued. Bethlehem Steel, Republic,
Inland, Youngstown Sheet and Tube — known together as
Little Steel — held out. In May the steelworkers struck —
Lewis said afterward without consulting him. The companies fought the strike with guards, spies, munitions, with
back-to-work ads, police harassment and violence. They
organized citizens' committees to recruit strikebreakers and
to organize community demonstrations backing the companies' antiunion stand. The American Iron and Steel
Institute trumpeted its defiance of the advancing SWOC;
it would oppose "any attempt to compel its employees to
join a union or pay tribute for the right to work" — the
traditional war cry of the open shop. President Roosevelt
appeared indifferent. In the end, the strike wasted away.
Two companies signed face-saving memoranda. The others
yielded nothing. The CIO was wounded, its onrush
momentarily stayed.

It was slowed, too, by a sharp recession. Unemployment hit the new unions with special force. The CIO laid
off half its organizing staff. It struggled to hold the
membership it had, put less emphasis on gaining new.
Lewis repeatedly underscored unemployment as the central
problem of the time. He called on labor to take up the
task of asserting the claim of the poor and the jobless to
a part "in the bounties and the blessings, material and
otherwise, in our country which are ample for the provision of all."

When the CIO leaders met in 1937 at their annual

conference, they claimed a membership of four million. It is difficult, says a major labor historian, "to exaggerate the achievements of the CIO in its first two years. . . . The successful drives of the CIO forced the AFL to follow suit." That spring, William Green had commented that "the country seems to be filled with CIO organizers." But the ranks of AFL organizers had been growing, too. It had 35 on its staff in early 1937; a year later, 232. It spent $82,000 on organizing in the fall of 1936; by the fall of 1937, it was spending nearly half a million dollars. It, too, was expanding. Even the unions that had most vigorously fought the craft unions' battle — the carpenters and machinists — were organizing on industrial lines. Under the impact of the parallel drives, union membership in the U. S. climbed to 7,200,000 in 1937 — an increase over the year before of over 3,000,000. It continued to climb, in 1941 passing the 10,000,000 mark — most of that growth in the resurgent AFL. Despite repeated efforts, no ground for uniting the two federations could be found. They were divided by widely differing backgrounds, by animosity and envy, by the very language they spoke. In 1938, the split was underscored; the Committee for Industrial Organization became the Congress of Industrial Organizations, intended as a permanent and continuing trade union center.

Lewis for many years had been a Republican. He had supported Hoover in 1928 and 1932. At one point, it was reported, he had been offered a seat in a Republican cabinet. However, he became an ardent supporter of Roosevelt's New Deal and a major figure in the campaign to reelect him in 1936. Early in the year he announced the formation of Labor's Nonpartisan League — in part in answer to the Democratic Party's appointment of the AFL's

Dan Tobin as its labor chairman. The league campaigned vigorously for FDR, though not for the Democrats as such. For a while George L. Berry, head of the AFL pressmen's politically minded union, headed the league. After he withdrew, it became the vehicle of the CIO, with Lewis and Sidney Hillman, the politically minded president of the Amalgamated Clothing Workers, as its dominant figures. It raised sizable sums of money for the campaign, the miners alone contributing nearly half a million dollars. Lewis had no intention of letting FDR forget it.

When the auto workers were hip-deep in battle with General Motors, Lewis looked to the White House for help. The very same economic royalists who had attacked the administration, he said, now have their fangs in labor. FDR replied that it was no time for conversation and headlines. Again, in the course of the Little Steel strike, Lewis had indicated that the workers expected the administration's help. FDR — undoubtedly irritated by a long and crowded season of sitdowns and walkouts — pronounced "a plague o' both their houses." Lewis held his reply until Labor Day, then exploded:

"Labor, like Israel, has many sorrows. Its women weep for the fallen and they lament for the future of the children of the race. It ill behooves one who has supped at labor's table and who has been sheltered in labor's house to curse with equal fervor and fine impartiality both labor and its adversaries when they become locked in deadly embrace."

In 1938, Lewis told the miners' convention that FDR had been "the only President in our lifetime who has tried to give a square deal to the common people." It was perhaps the last time Lewis would praise him. He turned down an invitation that year to take part in the

President's birthday celebration, which was devoted to raising funds to combat polio. "I am fully occupied," he said, "in trying to get consideration and work relief and money for the millions now unemployed in labor's ranks."

Lewis nursed his growing grudge; President Roosevelt tried to thread his way delicately between the two powerful and competing federations. Lewis demanded an undying loyalty — if not to him, then to the CIO, though at the time the AFL probably was the larger of the two. Lewis complained that FDR demanded support but gave little in return. Lewis objected that Roosevelt had selected Sidney Hillman as the labor man in the national defense program without consulting him. Most of all, they differed on the nation's foreign policy. Lewis objected to Roosevelt's defense preparations, to his support of the anti-Axis powers in Europe. He increasingly argued that Americans must avoid foreign involvement, must avoid any part in foreign wars. In this policy, Lewis had strong support from the left wing (including the Communist bloc) that held a prominent place in the CIO.

To the miners' Golden Jubilee convention in 1940, Lewis predicted FDR's "ignominious defeat" in his try for a third term. On October 25, in a nationwide radio broadcast, Lewis came out for FDR's opponent, Wendell Willkie. Roosevelt's reelection, he said, would be "a national evil." But if Roosevelt were reelected, Lewis vowed, "it will mean that members of the Congress of Industrial Organizations have rejected my advice and recommendations. I will accept the result as being the equivalent of a vote of no confidence, and will retire as President of the Congress of Industrial Organizations at its convention in November."

So, late in November, Lewis came to Atlantic City prepared to resign as head of the CIO. It also seems likely that he had considered the possibility that he would not be permitted to step down. Signs and posters urged him to change his mind, to stay on. A lengthy demonstration greeted his appearance. No one seemed to want to mention what was on everybody's mind. At that point, Sidney Hillman — a member then of the National Defense Advisory Commission, who shared FDR's policy differences with Lewis — spoke to the convention. He said simply that he regretted to see Lewis leave, but he was sure "that when John L. Lewis steps down there must be a demand for Phil Murray." Lewis himself nominated Murray; there was no opposition.

Lewis told the delegates — and many wept: "The poet said 'Who ascends to the mountain's top finds the loftiest peaks encased in mist and snow.' I think that is true. It is just as true in the ranks of labor. . . . That is the way of men and life, and we cannot stop to weep and wear sackcloth and ashes because something that happened yesterday did not meet with our approval, or that we did not have a dream come true. Tomorrow is the day that always faces men and women. . . ." He seemed, Saul Alinsky commented, "a man preaching his own funeral eulogy."

In the summer of 1941, Hitler turned against the Soviet Union. The CIO's left wing executed a sharp about-face. Now it — a longtime, vigorous supporter — turned against Lewis. That fall, when the CIO met again, Lewis and Phil Murray differed sharply on the course of the nation's foreign policy. They ended their friendship of many years' standing. Later, Lewis sat in the hotel dining room and pointed out the table — and the seating at the table — where a handful of men six years before had agreed to form a committee on industrial organization. "Here I conceived and built the CIO," Lewis said, "and it is here that I leave it." Within a year, the United Mine Workers withdrew from the CIO.

CHAPTER NINE

Sidney Hillman

"No child will cry for food
in the midst of plenty"

ONE CHICAGO clothing manufacturer deliberately hired newly arrived immigrants — " 'greenhorns,' Italian people, Jewish people . . . these I get for less wages," he said, about the turn of the century. The shops were dirty, cluttered, unsanitary: "no stable loft too foul," Jane Addams of Hull House said, "no rear shanty too provisional, no tenement room too small." The girls worked ten, twelve, fourteen hours a day; most of them took work home to earn a few extra pennies. Still they were paid only three to six dollars a week. In September, 1910, a handful of girls at the big Hart, Schaffner and Marx plant finally rebelled. They left their jobs and started picketing the plant. Slowly, then in swelling numbers, the other workers joined them. Soon, more than seven thousand were on strike.

When their own union, the United Garment Workers, offered little help or leadership, the strikers themselves carried their story to the people of Chicago. They won the support of the Chicago Federation of Labor, of the Women's Trade Union League, of Jane Addams and her friends at Hull House, of ministers and rabbis and news-papers. Doctors offered free medical services, coal dealers provided fuel; the gas company kept the gas on despite the unpaid bills and barbers cut the strikers' hair without charge. Suddenly, Thomas Rickert, president of the United Garment Workers, issued a strike call to all Chicago clothing workers, and they responded by the thousands. Almost as suddenly, Rickert announced a settlement with Hart, Schaffner and Marx. When the strikers learned that it did not recognize their union, they turned it down. One of the cutters, a curly-haired young man by the name of Sidney Hillman, the accent of the old country still thick in his speech, led the fight against it. He led the fight, too, that surrounded the visit of the IWW leader, Big Bill Haywood. Hillman insisted Haywood have a chance to speak; when nobody else would oppose him, Hillman did.

A picket was killed, and ten thousand strikers marched in his funeral cortege — "in a strange and frightening silence. No dirge sounded and not an outcry was heard." Joseph Schaffner, a founder of the business, was shocked by the strike; right up to the eve of the walkout he had assumed conditions were satisfactory. But he was even more shocked by the outcry of the city's union leaders, the clergy, the newspapers. "This strike is killing me," he told a friend. He finally agreed that all strikers could return to their jobs without discrimination. An arbitration committee would investigate their complaints and — even more important — would develop a method of adjusting grievances in the future. This time, Hillman fought for acceptance. At that moment, too, Rickert called off the precipitate strike of the other clothing workers; they went back to work under the old "miserable conditions." The

142

Amalgamated Clothing Workers of America

SIDNEY HILLMAN

Hart, Schaffner coatmakers asked Hillman to represent them. They pledged him ten dollars a week and a dollar for expenses.

Hillman was then just twenty-four. He had arrived in Chicago four years before. He had been born in 1887 in a small village in Lithuania, the second son among the seven children of a "stiff-necked" grain dealer and a hardworking mother. His father spent hours in the synagogue; his mother ran a small grocery store, kept a cow and sold the milk, managed a small bakery. Sidney was an intense, quiet boy — a "deep one," the rabbi called him. When five, he attended Bible school, becoming so absorbed in the lore of the Bible that, on one occasion, his classmates stripped his coat of its buttons without his knowing. He was chosen to carry on the family's rabbinical tradition — a decision he credited for his own devotion to the union movement. "The rabbis in our family were . . . the rank-and-file kind that are called upon more to help than to lead," he recalled. "Concern in the everyday problems of working people was their job, so I took it for granted it had to be mine."

When he was fourteen (in 1901), he was sent to the yeshiva — the rabbinical school — at Kovno. He was a shy, skinny youngster, fascinated by his first glimpses of a larger world. He had only six rubles a month for his food allowance, barely enough for a piece of bread, some pickles, a slice of herring and tea. His day began at sunrise, ended at sunset, the hours between devoted to study of Hebrew, the Scriptures, the Talmud. Soon, even this world seemed narrow. He longed to study the Russian language, literature, mathematics, but these were strictly forbidden. A friend, Michael Zacharias, arranged lessons for him nonetheless at the home of his uncle, Dr. Matis, and his

144

aunt. Twice each week, Sidney walked the three miles
to their house for instruction. Both the yeshiva and his
father objected. When Sidney refused to give up the lessons,
his father cut off his allowance. The boy went to live with
Dr. Matis, earning his way by working in his laboratory.
He felt even more rewarded when he was taken into the
miniature "university" formed by the doctor and his young
friends. Systematically, they explored science, sociology,
economics. Inevitably the group became involved in the
political agitation for democratic rights that in 1905 was
stirring Russia. Sidney carried messages for underground
political workers. He helped to organize the typesetters in
Kovno; one of his jobs was to carry the group's hecto-
graph, on which they printed their propaganda, from house
to house to avoid having it confiscated by the police. When
he was seventeen, he led a parade of workers down Kovno's
main street. The demonstration was promptly broken up,
and young Hillman was arrested and jailed.

His companions in prison, he quickly learned, were
political prisoners too, jailed for demanding democratic
rights from a tyrannical czar. The prisoners spent hours in
open cells, talking and arguing, reading and exchanging
books on political economy and the rights of man. Sidney
was released after five months. Soon he was arrested again
for distributing handbills, but freed four months later in
a general pardon. Finally, as the czarist police pressed in
on the revolutionary movement, he obtained a forged pass-
port and left the country. He stayed a short time with
an uncle in Liverpool, then in 1907 joined the swelling
wave of emigration to America. He paused briefly in New
York, then at the invitation of his old friend, Michael
Zacharias, went on to Chicago.

There he found a job as a stock clerk at Sears Roebuck.

His spare moments were spent reading one book after another from a nearby library. In the panic of 1907, he was fired. He always remembered the fear he had seen in the eyes of his fellow employees at Sears. Their constant worry, he recalled, was who would be next. He once offered to exchange places with an older family man who was being fired; the other employees told him it would do no good — his place would merely be filled by a boy receiving even less than he. After a time, he was hired at Hart, Schaffner and Marx as a cutter's apprentice. He worked six weeks without pay learning the trade, then was paid six dollars a week. After a year he was earning eight dollars a week. A colleague once remarked that Sidney Hillman "if I may say so, was a damn poor cutter."

In the first months after the strike, the plant was racked by short strikes, impatient workers, angry supervisors, unsettled grievances. Schaffner appointed Professor Earl Dean Howard of Northwestern University as his labor-relations manager. Together, he and Hillman ranged the plant, taking up complaints on the spot. What grievances could not be settled between them went to the "trade board," made up of five employer and five employee representatives. If the board was unable to agree, the problem was referred to an arbitration board; the decision of its neutral chairman, the patient John E. Williams, was final. The machinery worked with increasing efficiency to ease the tension and restore peace in the plant. Its pattern for settling disputes also marked a major milestone in the course of the nation's industrial relations.

For his part in making the plan work, Hillman won widespread respect. Schaffner thought he was "the squarest labor leader I have ever known." In January, 1914, he was invited to become chief clerk for the Ladies Garment

Workers in New York — the same job as at Hart, Schaffner and Marx at about three times the salary. He left Chicago with a new watch, the gift of the shop chairmen at Hart, Schaffner, and with a secret engagement to Bessie Abramowitz, one of the girls whose picket lines touched off the Hart, Schaffner and Marx strike.

Hillman and the Ladies Garment Workers in New York did not hit it off. To some he seemed an outsider. Others thought him too conservative. Political conflicts within the unions and the rising dissatisfaction of the employers hindered the complaint-handling procedure that had been set up under the pioneering Protocol of Peace a few years before.

Meantime, revolt was bubbling up in the United Garment Workers. The New York tailors, unhappy with Rickert's interference in their strike in 1912, were determined to oust him. The still resentful Chicago members were eager to assist. To fend off their challenge, Rickert set the union's convention at Nashville, Tennessee, a deliberately out-of-the-way location. He billed the dissident locals for some $75,000 in dues, insisting they must be paid before the delegates would be seated. On the second morning, 107 delegates were barred from the convention floor. Together with the Chicago delegation, they met in separate session. As a majority of the delegates, they insisted they constituted the real union convention. That night, talk in their caucuses turned to Hillman. In the small hours of the morning they sent him a telegram: YOU MUST ACCEPT PRESIDENCY. WE ARE THE MAJORITY SO DECIDE AND WIRE AT ONCE." Hillman talked it over with some friends. One objected that it would cost him his reputation. As a friend recalled it, Hillman replied: "I owe my present 'standing' to the tailors. I was no great shakes when I walked the Chicago streets some six or seven years ago in search of a nine-dollar-a-week apprentice-cutter job. The tailors, it seems, need me now, and they should have me — and that standing, too."

Gompers refused to recognize the insurgents as the majority of the United Garment Workers; he told them they should have fought out their complaints, however serious, inside the union. They replied that there was no effective way open to them. Finally, in December, 1914, they met in convention and formed their own, independent union — the Amalgamated Clothing Workers of America. Almost before the last speech had been made, the new union was involved in conflict; it fought strikes and lockouts, jurisdictional disputes and lawsuits with the former union and even the IWW, and an AFL boycott. Slowly, though, in the face of trouble and strife, the union extended its reach.

In the midst of the new union's fight for survival, Hillman was guest of honor at a banquet in Chicago. He used the occasion to announce his forthcoming marriage to Bessie Abramowitz. Hand in hand, they led the May Day parade of clothing workers, then spent their honeymoon at the Amalgamated's second convention. Bessie gave up her job as business agent of Local 152, but she has remained close to the union ever since.

By the end of World War I the Amalgamated represented some 100,000 clothing workers. It renewed its old battles — against sweatshop employers, the open shop, against depression and bankruptcy in the industry. More and more, Hillman talked of driving out chiseling and inefficiency, of raising standards — not merely for the union members but for the whole industry. "We cannot wreck the house in which we expect to live," he said. He used industrial engineers to measure the speed of work, to help set piece rates, to improve efficiency. The union nursed sick firms back to health, installing cost systems, eliminating waste motion, cutting unnecessary overhead. In one instance among many, the Amalgamated loaned an employer $100,000 to take over a plant. The loan saved the jobs of some nine hundred union members. Back of his concern with efficiency was the idea that "we cannot ask from industry more than it can soundly afford to give."

Hillman led the Amalgamated in exploring new and pioneering union services. First in Chicago, later in Rochester and New York, the union set up unemployment insurance funds. In 1922, the Amalgamated opened its own bank in Chicago, and a second in New York less than a year later. The Amalgamated banks were run with the caution and conservatism of a small-town banker. When the depression began to lift in the early 1930s, only the two Amalgamated banks among some thirty-five union-sponsored banks had survived.

Hillman organized a relief ship that carried a quarter of a million dollars of food, clothing and drugs to famine-stricken Russia. He raised money to finance several clothing factories in the Soviet Union at a time when major American firms — Ford, General Electric and others — were also providing help. The Soviet government eventually took control of the plants after refunding the investments of American stockholders.

In the midtwenties, the union bought land in the northern end of the Bronx and built an impressive housing development. It provided bright new homes for some three hundred Amalgamated families, the first of a series of Amalgamated projects offering attractive new housing to hundreds of clothing workers and their families.

During the twenties, too, Hillman fought off efforts of the Communists to take over the union. He met their demands with a continued militance of his own and with the union's expanding social program. The Communists were entitled to try to make a revolution, he commented, but they can't expect us to deliver the union to them. Racketeers captured control of a key cutters' local in New York. Hillman led a parade of notable citizens to New York's City Hall, protesting the gangsters' threats and intimidation and violence. The mayor pledged the full support of his police force to maintain the peace. Hillman fought back with a series of strikes aimed at isolating the gangster-controlled firms. Then, backed by the general executive board, Hillman's cohorts ousted the local's top officers and took physical control of its office and books. The ousted officers went to court in an effort to stave off the Amalgamated take-over, but the court refused to interfere.

By 1932, though, the industry was running at less than a third of capacity. The union's membership had fallen in a few years by over 50,000. The union's unemployment insurance funds could contribute only a few dollars a week, and then only in limited areas. Wages were cut, sometimes by half. Sweatshops hired youngsters at ten and fifteen cents an hour.

To end the depression, to restore jobs and prosperity, Hillman called for a national economic council, with capital and labor and the public sharing the nation's major economic decisions. The government need not stand by helplessly, he argued; it must take the lead in providing jobs, raising wages, expanding production. "Start the wheels of industry going by priming from the bottom, not from the top," he urged. His was one among many proposals for government action that led, early in Franklin Delano Roosevelt's first term, to the National Industrial Recovery Act. Hillman served on a labor committee that helped write the bill. He was made a member of the Labor Advisory Committee after the bill was passed. To him, its key provision was Section 7(a), the recognition of the workers' right to organize and bargain collectively. But it would help little, he warned, unless labor took full advantage of the new sanction. (Even before the NRA became law, the Amalgamated launched a sweeping organizing drive.)

As a member of the NRA Labor Advisory Committee, Hillman worked to raise the level of minimum wages and reduce the hours of work in the industry codes. His efforts were not always successful, but to critics Hillman counseled, "We must use the instruments that are at hand." With the NRA floundering, Administrator Hugh Johnson quit. In his place, Roosevelt named a seven-man board and made Hillman the labor member. Almost before the board could swing into action, the Supreme Court held the NRA unconstitutional. Hillman packed his bags to return to New York. He vowed he would raise a million dollars to help protect the gains labor had won under the ill-fated program. "We're going to need it," he said.

From the start of the New Deal, Hillman and John L. Lewis became friends. With Lewis' help, the Amalgamated signed a peace treaty with the United Garment Workers and was admitted to the AFL in the fall of 1933. At Atlantic City in 1935, Hillman lined up solidly behind Lewis and the industrial-union supporters. He was among the small group in the hotel dining room that made the final plans for launching the CIO. When the "Committee" became the Congress in 1938, Lewis nominated Hillman for vice-president. "Hillman wrote the lines of the play and Lewis acted them," commented one union leader. To the AFL at one point, Lewis was "the dominating and fulminating Caesar," Hillman "the Machiavelli" of the CIO. Hillman stood alongside Lewis when they organized Labor's Nonpartisan League to back FDR in 1936. At Hillman's urging, the Amalgamated contributed $100,000 to the campaign.

In March of 1937, the CIO launched still another massive organizing drive — this one under the Textile Workers Organizing Committee, with Hillman at its head and the Amalgamated footing a large share of the bill. He sent a force of six hundred and fifty organizers into the textile centers. Their efforts produced some results, though the going was rough in the antiunion South. TWOC signed up thousands, even so, obtained pledges from thousands more, and signed hundreds of agreements. It was brought to a sharp standstill, though, by the recession of 1937.

At that critical moment, Hillman fell ill. For days, his life was in danger. He recovered and went off to Florida to regain his strength. Five months passed before he was able to return to active duty. During his long recuperation, he became convinced that labor must seek a national law putting a floor under wages and a ceiling over hours. It was a necessary defense for organized industries against low-wage, nonunion competition. Lewis gladly gave him the job of obtaining such a law. The bill proposed a minimum wage of twenty-five cents an hour to start with, rising to forty cents; it proposed a maximum of forty-four hours a week, reducing to forty. Hillman mounted an intensive drive to line up support — in the White House as well as in Congress. On June 14, 1938, the minimum wage and maximum hour bill became law. Both FDR and Lewis gave Hillman much of the credit. "If it had not been for him," Lewis said, "there would probably have been no Fair Labor Standards Act."

As the differences grew between Lewis and Roosevelt, Hillman was called on more frequently to serve as go-between. But differences were also developing between Hillman and Lewis over the rising foreign crisis. Lewis attacked a third term for Roosevelt at the miners' Golden Jubilee convention; Hillman reminded the miners of their gains under the New Deal. At the Amalgamated's Silver Anniversary convention, Lewis again challenged the Roosevelt policies; the delegates, though, under Hillman's leadership, enthusiastically endorsed a third term. That summer, Roosevelt named Hillman to the National Defense Advisory Commission. Lewis considered the appointment an affront. Had he at least been approached, he said, he would have endorsed the appointment. Later, Lewis added that the appointment was part of Roosevelt's efforts to "wean away the primary loyalty of many of my lieutenants." Hillman worked even harder for FDR's reelection; Lewis finally burst out in anger and defiance: if FDR were reelected, he declared, he would resign as head of the CIO.

Hillman had not planned to attend the CIO convention after the election. But Lewis' left-wing supporters, sharing his opposition to FDR's foreign policies, were mounting an intensive campaign to keep Lewis on the job. Phil Murray was hesitant about replacing his longtime friend. Hillman stepped into the breach. Lewis declared the issue was not war, but "fifty-two million shrunken bellies." Hillman asked the convention "where is free labor in France? In concentration camps. . . . Bombs are exploding in the workmen's sections in every part of Britain. . . . Who wants to live in a world dominated by scoundrels?" Lewis had blocked an anti-Communist resolution introduced by Amalgamated delegates. Hillman pointed to the anti-Communist bars in the Mine Workers' bylaws. "What is good enough for the Mine Workers is good enough for me." He went on: "I regret that John L. Lewis will not be the leader of this organization . . . it is my considered judgment that when John L. Lewis steps down there must be a demand for Phil Murray." Reported *The New York Times:* "Hillman coldly, logically killed any hopes for a draft-Lewis movement." Hillman later explained: "It just came to me while I was up there talking."

In his defense job, President Roosevelt told Hillman, he was responsible for the labor policy of the whole national defense program. Hillman set up an advisory committee made up of representatives of the AFL, CIO and railroad brotherhoods. "We meet regularly," he noted. "What is more to the point, we agree regularly." Under his direction, a training program took shape to meet shortages of skilled labor that were bound to develop as the defense program expanded. He worked to steer defense contracts away from firms that violated the National Labor Relations (the Wagner) Act. He protested a contract awarded Ford, which was then resisting the auto workers at every step. He persuaded Roosevelt to question contracts awarded Bethlehem Steel and other firms. In the midst of the controversy, Roosevelt abolished the National Defense Advisory Committee, substituted the Office of Production Management. He made General Motors' William H. Knudsen director-general, and Hillman his associate. Critics questioned whether OPM could operate effectively under two-headed rule. FDR answered for the two men: "I think they will. They think they will."

In OPM, Hillman was charged with coordinating manpower supply and enforcing labor standards. He helped to avert strikes in defense plants; when they could not be averted, he helped to settle them. Lewis called him a traitor for supporting Roosevelt's decision to send troops to take over the strikebound North American airplane plant. "What is right today may be wrong tomorrow," Hillman replied. He pointed out that the British were being driven back, Yugoslavia had surrendered, the Japanese were pushing into South Asia. Hillman took a hand, too, in encouraging a policy of fair employment for workers of all colors and creeds.

When war came, the President wiped out OPM and created the War Production Board. He put Donald M. Nelson at the head of it; Hillman expected to head its labor division. Then, without advance word of any kind, the manpower responsibility was handed to a War Manpower Commission, and Hillman, bitterly disappointed, was out. "Once the most powerful labor man in government," an AFL official wrote, "he was at his 'nadir' from which it was generally believed he could not rise politically. Even at the White House he was in eclipse as big businessmen gained more influence and obtained strategic positions." Whatever his personal status, though, he turned over to the new organization a broad foundation for building wartime manpower and labor policies.

At that moment, Hillman suffered a severe heart attack — almost as if, one doctor suggested, he took the full blow of his disappointment in his heart. The President urged him to stay on as a special assistant on labor matters. Hillman felt keenly that FDR's confidence in him had weakened. He could do more, he thought, by returning to the Amalgamated.

More than a year later, Phil Murray asked him to head a political action group in the CIO. Hillman was enthusiastic. The CIO Political Action Committee was organized in the summer of 1943 to mobilize the votes of millions of CIO members, farm and consumer groups, church and community organizations. Through political action, it hoped to give the nation's ordinary people a voice in the nation's political decisions, in determining the peace, in planning for the postwar period. With the slogan, "Every worker a voter," PAC mounted intensive drives to register voters. "One thing we know in the labor movement," Hillman enthusiastically commented, "is organization."

PAC moved into the district, among others, of Martin Dies, head of the House Un-American Activities Committee. Dies threatened to expose PAC's income and expenditures and later published a report charging that Hillman was building PAC "by entering into a coalition with the Communists." Hillman flatly accused Dies of lying. Faced with a growing and unfriendly registration, Dies withdrew from the race and gave up his seat in Congress. It was CIO-PAC's first victory.

When the Democratic convention met in Chicago in the summer of 1944, Hillman and CIO-PAC were reported to have two hundred delegates under their direction. Whatever the actual number, both Hillman and Murray were determined to have a say in choosing FDR's running mate; he could, quite conceivably, be the next President. CIO-PAC's first choice was Vice-President Henry Wallace, but Hillman told FDR it would not oppose Senator Harry Truman. The President wavered between Wallace and Truman, gave consideration to James F. Byrnes and Supreme Court Justice William O. Douglas. As time for the decision neared, FDR was reported to have advised one of his representatives that, in making a final choice, he must first "clear it with Sidney." The phrase was reported in *The New York Times* and echoed for months afterward. Westbrook Pegler, the angry and sometimes venomous columnist, exploded: "Hillman! In God's name! How came this non-toiling sedentary conspirator who never held American office or worked in the Democratic organization to give orders to the Democrats of the United States?" The phrase echoed in the campaign. A Republican poster asked: "It's your country. Why let Sidney Hillman run it?" More than one observer doubted that FDR ever said anything of the sort; few doubted, though, that Hillman, Murray and CIO-PAC played an important part in the convention's decision. Few doubted, either, the vigor and enthusiasm and effective organization that the CIO-PAC forces brought to the campaign. FDR greeted Hillman after the election: "One thing I want to make perfectly clear to Sidney is my appreciation." The CIO convention that November gave Hillman a half-hour ovation.

As the war drew to a close, Hillman worked on behalf of the CIO to form the World Federation of Trade Unions. He was instrumental in bringing both the Russians and the British into the organization. At one point, the AFL was the only major national trade union center outside the WFTU.

On the closing day of the Amalgamated convention in 1946, a reporter sent a note to the rostrum. "Would Sidney Hillman . . . set forth a little of his philosophy about the kind of world American labor was seeking to create?"

> We want a better America [Hillman responded], that will give its citizens, first of all, a higher and higher standard of living, so that no child will cry for food in the midst of plenty. We want to have

an America where the inventions of science will be at the disposal of every American family, not merely for the few who can afford them. An America that . . . will make it possible for groups regardless of race, creed, or color to live in friendship . . . an America that will carry on its great mission of helping other countries to help themselves.

Some years before, Hillman had urged an Amalgamated convention: ". . . let us not become too practical. Having realized our dreams of yesterday, let us dedicate ourselves to new dreams of a future where there will be no unemployment; a future where men and women will be economically secure and politically free. Let us dream these dreams and let us . . . dedicate ourselves to make these dreams a reality."

In June, 1946, he suffered still another heart attack. He rested for several weeks, then returned to his office. Leaving early that day, he paused to look at the Amalgamated Bank's newly refurbished offices. "The tailors have come a long way," he mused. He died the next morning. "He had never really halted to catch his breath," wrote his biographer, Matthew Josephson, "or renew his waning strength, continuing in full career to the very end — all anxiety and zeal and hope."

CHAPTER TEN

David Dubinsky

"There was so much to be done"

SHE WAS only "a wisp of a girl still in her teens." Facing her from the platform were a number of impressive personalities of the day: Sam Gompers, head of the American Federation of Labor; Mary Dreier, president of the Women's Trade Union League, an organization of wealthy, socially prominent, socially minded New York women; leaders in the Socialist Party, then winning increasing political influence; top officials of the International Ladies Garment Workers Union. Surrounding her were some two thousand shirtwaist makers — like herself, young, impatient, determined. The cautious, indecisive speeches had droned on for two hours when young Clara Lemlich raised her hand, "I am a working girl," she cried in angry Yiddish, "one of those who are on strike against intolerable conditions. I am tired of listening to speakers who talk in general terms. What we are here for is to decide whether we shall or shall not strike. I offer a resolution that a general strike be declared — now." The meeting burst into bedlam; the audience came to its feet, cheering, shouting, waving umbrellas or hats or whatever came to hand. The chairman asked if they would keep the faith. Two thousand young voices joined in the vow: "If I turn traitor to the cause I now pledge, may this hand wither from the arm I raise." So in November, 1909, began the uprising of the twenty thousand shirtwaist makers.

Even while the shirtwaist makers fought for life, the cloakmakers of New York faced their own struggle. They collected a two-dollar strike tax, prepared the ground with bulletins published in English, Yiddish and Italian. On July 7, some fifty — perhaps sixty — thousand cloakmakers answered the strike call. So in July, 1910, began the great revolt of the cloakmakers. Peace had hardly returned to the industry when — in March, 1911 — fire swept the Triangle Shirtwaist Company "with its locked doors, collapsing fire escape, non-operating hoses and 146 dead" — and this in the face of a warning delivered only a month earlier against the terrible danger of fire.

In these brief, stark moments, public attention focused on a world that few outsiders knew. It was the world of the immigrant, the "greenhorn"; of the new ghettos and of a dark, desperate struggle to survive. They had fled, hundreds of thousands each year, from the cruelty of Old World tyrannies — from the Jewish ghettos of Russia, the impoverished villages of Italy, every corner of Europe. They fled from hunger and ignorance, from cruel and abrasive poverty. They came, as it turned out, to new ghettos and merciless exploitation — to the dirty, crowded, disease-ridden sweatshops, to long hours and low pay, to airless, squalid tenements. And yet — they clung to the conviction that America would, in fact, be a land of opportunity, that their children would see a better life than they had known. In their baggage they had brought a vast miscellany of ideas and philosophies and creeds. Some were veterans

Jerry Soalt for ILGWU "Justice"

DAVID DUBINSKY

of Old World revolts, experienced in underground political fighting. Some were educated, some were illiterate. The sweatshop brought them together. Out of their agony, slowly, painfully, they built the International Ladies Garment Workers Union.

The striking shirtwaist makers fought through the cold, bitter winter of 1909-10. Police and magistrates endlessly harassed them and hunger hounded them. The public was stunned by the sweatshops in which they worked and the tenements in which they lived. In February, 1910, their strike ended — not with victory but with substantial gains. Now their employers — not the girls — would pay for the needles, the thread, the very electric power they used in their work. They won a fifty-two-hour week and the right to share equally in what work was available during the slack season. The employers agreed to set piece rates jointly with the workers' representatives. The cloakmakers, too, fought through eight weeks of injunctions and picket-line violence and "grim hostility." Their settlement in September, 1910, was worked out with the help of the well-known Jewish leader, Louis Marshall, and of Louis D. Brandeis, the Boston lawyer who would one day sit on the nation's highest court. It came to be known as the Protocol of Peace. Along with some sizable improvements in the cloakmakers' jobs, it made two unique contributions. One was the grievance machinery that provided a series of steps — negotiations, then conciliation, finally arbitration — for settling employer-employee disputes. It was over this pattern that the Hart, Schaffner and Marx plan was cut some months later. The protocol also set up a Joint Board of Sanitary Control. Its job was to establish standards of sanitation in the workshops as the first step toward eliminating the miserable sweatshop. It was a report of the

162

Joint Board early in 1911 that had warned of the widespread lack of fire protection in the garment shops. The outrage that followed the Triangle Shirtwaist Company fire a month later led to a factory investigating commission and, in turn, to far-reaching reforms in factory inspection and safety laws. Beyond these results — at the bottom of them — was the establishment of the union as a factor of weight and consequence in the industry.

Important as it was, the protocol died or was killed — partly because it was often clumsy and slow in its working; partly because unions and employers differed on its desirability. It died, finally, when the employers locked out some 25,000 workers in April, 1916. In retaliation, the union called a general strike in the industry. The union not only survived the lockout, but actually made distinct gains. The grievance machinery of the protocol was discarded, though the industry would return to something of its ideas and principles in later years. It was in that strike and lockout that a short, stocky young cutter by the name of David Dubinsky set out on his union career.

Like many of his fellow garment workers, David was a newcomer. He had arrived in New York on New Year's Day, 1911. He had been born eighteen years before (on February 22) in the city of Brest-Litovsk in the Russia of the czars. He grew up in the town of Lodz in Russian Poland where his father ran a small bakery. Lodz was an ugly, dirty industrial city, its factories and slums carelessly mingled among the palaces of the rich. Dirty water flowed along the streets, often strangely colored by the dyes in the waste water from nearby textile factories. Here, at 16 Vschodnia Street, David spent his boyhood.

There were three short, restless years at school, but at eleven he turned to learning the baker's trade. By the time he was fourteen, he was rated a "master" baker. It was a harsh trade, the hours long, the wages poor. He joined the Bund — the General Jewish Workers Union. It was, at that time, an illegal organization and carried on its work secretly. Almost at once, he was made assistant secretary of the bakers' union — he was considered "quite a scholar," because he could read and write and keep books. "And keeping books," he told a biographer, "was just as important to the bakers in Lodz as it is in the International today." He helped to organize a strike — against his father's shop, too — and the bakers won a small increase. But the next night most of the strike leaders, including young David, were arrested. He was released after two weeks when his father paid the local police chief twenty-five rubles and agreed David would leave Lodz.

After an impatient three months with an uncle at Brest, David returned. One of the first men he met was Ivan, a strike leader and secretary of the bakers. "I don't know you," he told David. "Please leave me alone." Later, David recalled, "He was through. We never saw him again. Hundreds of good men were broken like that almost overnight." Next day, the fifteen-year-old boy was made secretary of the union. Soon, though, the police raided an illegal meeting, and he was arrested a second time. This time, he was sentenced to exile in a small Siberian village under police surveillance. En route, he spent month after month in one prison after another, much of the time with friendly and helpful burglars and thieves. They explained their friendliness on the ground that the "political" prisoners sacrificed themselves for "everybody." He also met other "politicals" and spent long hours in political and economic arguments. In the course of a transfer from one prison to the village where he was to serve out his exile, he managed to run away. Peasants befriended him, then sped him on his way; other exiles took him in. His father finally sent him money to return to Lodz. There he went back to work at his old trade but under an assumed name. His older brother, by then in America, sent him a ticket. With his second brother, he stole across the border, crossed Germany and sailed for the United States.

His first job in New York was washing dishes in a neighborhood diner. When he was offered a chance to learn the garment cutter's trade, he grabbed it. He paid a substantial fee to the foreman who taught him the trade; he faced a tough test from the union examiners. But six months after his arrival, he obtained a card in the Cutters' Union, Local 10 of the ILGWU. The Socialist Party became his first interest. He developed his skills in using the language in party activities — principally in a cooperative group that ran restaurants, a boardinghouse, a grocery store. There, he met Emma Goldberg, a garment worker and a member of Local 62. They were married in 1914. Though he himself was on strike, it was as a Socialist that he became active in the 1916 lockout. Soon he found himself involved in the union's activities. He was elected to Local 10's executive board in 1918, to its vice-presidency in 1919 and in the next year, to its presidency. When the executive board decided to combine the three departments — coat and suit, waist, and dress — into one and put a general manager in charge, the job was offered to Dubinsky. In 1921, then just twenty-nine, he became general manager and secretary-treasurer of Local 10. "I wanted the job because there was so much to be done," he told a biographer, Benjamin Stolberg, and yet he hesitated. "I was afraid that I wasn't big enough." In 1923, he was elected to the ILGWU's general executive board.

Dubinsky's rise in the union almost paralleled the rise of the left wing. Many of the garment workers had come from the revolutionary movements and the radical political parties of the Old World. Many had known the tyranny of the czar and welcomed his overthrow by the Communists. In America, their energies spread over many radical philosophies and in many directions. Out of the political churning that marked the period following the First World War came a radical opposition in the union. It came under Communist leadership and launched a serious drive to capture control of the union. The International union leadership — first under Benjamin Schlessinger, even more vigorously under his successor, Morris Sigman — fought back. Local union leaders were expelled but often retained the backing of their local union membership. They acquired support in other local unions. The Communists called a general strike — a disastrous strike that lasted twenty-seven weeks, cost the union some $3,500,000, including over $800,000 in employers' bonds that had been left with the union as security for faithful performance. Both sides paid incredibly heavy prices to hire gangsters. The strike finally was settled on a piecemeal basis. The ousted leaders took their followers into a short-lived left-wing union, the Needle Trades Workers Industrial Union.

The cost had been high. "Our achievements have been lost," Dubinsky said. "The working conditions which we obtained at the price of a quarter century of struggle, sacrifices and hardships were nullified. Our membership dwindled down to less than half, and what is more, the morale of the members and the spirit even among some of the leadership reached the lowest ebb in our history."

Through the strife, the International had two major sources of strength: the Italian locals under the leadership of Luigi Antonini and Local 10 under Dubinsky. Local 10's strength was owing, in part at least, to a defeat Dubinsky himself had suffered at the hands of the opposition in 1924. Unhappy, disappointed, feeling he could no longer serve the union, Dubinsky decided to resign. He took out a working card and found a job. When word of his plans got around, cutters by the score urged him to stay. One, Dubinsky particularly remembered, came to him with tears in his eyes. "You have a duty to perform to us and that is to stay with the union." Dubinsky changed his mind; he also changed his tactics. Politics could work both ways; he organized the members of the union to counteract the activities of the opposition. He could not take their support for granted. It was the beginning of the almost total rout of the opposition in Local 10. In turn, it was the foundation of Local 10's support for the International union. When it was over, Dubinsky was widely accepted as a major figure in the union. In 1929, he was chosen secretary-treasurer of the International.

Then began a desperate effort to save the union. The two leaders — Schlessinger had been returned to the president's chair — collected special taxes from a dwindling membership. They floated reconstruction bonds. They persuaded three prominent New York financiers — Herbert H. Lehman, Julius Rosenwald, Felix M. Warburg — to lend the near-bankrupt union $100,000. They also faced a rapidly deepening depression. Thousands of garment workers were out of work, thousands more on part time. Garment manufacturers were fleeing to small towns in search of cheap labor. The union cut its staff, and those who remained drew five or ten dollars when there was money in the till. Often the phone was "temporarily disconnected" and the elevator "out of order" when the bills went un-

paid. In 1932, the union fell to its lowest point in a score
or more of years. In 1932, too, Schlessinger died. Dubinsky
was the obvious choice as his successor, but he hesitated.
He said he was fearful of the split in authority between
the president and the secretary-treasurer. The board found
a way around his objection: the office would be left vacant
until one candidate could command "substantial unanimity"; until then, Dubinsky would fill both jobs. On June 14,
1932, he became president as well as secretary-treasurer.

Even before the National Recovery Act became law,
the ILG swung into action. It called a strike in Philadelphia, won a 10 per cent increase and union recognition.
The Philadelphia walkout was a prelude to a great national
drive. With Section 7(a) back of it, the ILG campaign
unrolled in great waves, covering the coat and suit trade,
then the dress trade, finally the miscellaneous trades. The
NRA codes covering the ladies garment industries called for
a thirty-five-hour week, set minimum wage rates. They imposed new responsibilities on jobbers and contractors. At
the 1934 convention, Dubinsky reported that the membership had climbed from 45,000 to 200,000, that the debts
of the union had been paid off, that it now had assets
of more than $850,000 — including a half million dollars
in the bank. (On the second day of the convention, when
it was learned that the Medinah Club was making life
unpleasant for Negro delegates, the convention was packed
into a fleet of taxis and trucks and moved, lock, stock
and delegates, to the Morrison Hotel. Said Dubinsky, re-
opening the convention: "The ILG practices what it
preaches.") In 1934, too, Dubinsky was elected to the
executive council of the AFL.

When the Supreme Court knocked out the NRA,
Dubinsky reminded the members that the court decision

could not nullify their economic strength. He called on them to strike against any effort of employers, individually or together, to weaken the union or reduce its standards. In the coat and suit industry, the union and employers set up their own recovery board. It adopted the substance of the old NRA code and issued a consumer protection label to insure the maintenance of fair standards.

Dubinsky sided with the industrial union forces when that dispute hit the floor of the AFL conventions. He sat with Lewis in two of the preliminary sessions leading up to the CIO. He was one of the eight founders. There was an important difference. Dubinsky contended that the CIO should function inside the AFL. So long as that was its direction and purpose, Dubinsky was a convinced and enthusiastic supporter. He was the lone CIO member on the AFL executive council — Lewis had resigned in a huff at Green's first suggestion that the committee dissolve. His was frequently the lone voice raised in defense of the industrial-union organizing drive. He told his own executive board that, though he sometimes disagreed with the tone and approach of some CIO leaders, it was, nevertheless, "a movement with which the ILG has profound sympathy and whose objectives are close to the hearts of our members."

Dubinsky joined Lewis in supporting FDR in 1936, gave full backing to Labor's Nonpartisan League. In New York, it took the name of the American Labor Party and ILG vice-president Antonini was made state chairman. Dubinsky himself gave up his long — nearly twenty-five years' — affiliation with the Socialist Party to become a Roosevelt elector on the New York state ballot. (Later, Dubinsky and Hillman fought a no-holds-barred battle for control of the American Labor Party. Hillman won, and the Dubinsky forces withdrew to form their own Liberal Party.)

Meantime, expulsion of the ILG from the AFL was looming. Dubinsky gave up his seat on the executive council, and in time the union was ousted, along with the other CIO unions. Dubinsky took the stand that industrial unionism must be upheld, but dual unionism (two unions organizing workers in the same craft or industry) must be resisted. He became increasingly convinced that Lewis wanted no peace between the factions. There is, Dubinsky argued, "no longer any reason for prolonging this fratricidal conflict." He added — and everybody assumed he was pointing at Lewis, "No one has a mortgage on the labor movement and it is not the property of any individual or group." Lewis compared Dubinsky to "Eliza crossing the ice and looking backward." Dubinsky reminded him that Eliza was fleeing "none too kind an overseer." Despite Lewis' wisecracks, he went on, American workers want peace.

In the summer of 1938, Lewis announced the CIO would form a permanent organization. Dubinsky promptly declared that the ILG would have no part of it. He sent a team of his own people on a "peace mission" but its efforts were rejected. The ILG stayed away from the CIO's first constitutional convention, and it remained apart in what Dubinsky called "comfortable independence." It sent word to the AFL, though, that it would rejoin if the anti-CIO assessment were abolished, if the AFL would prohibit the Executive Council from suspending or expelling an affiliated union, and if it would take action against the racketeers in its own ranks. Green offered the ILG strong assurances on the first two points, passed over the third. On June 6, 1940, William Green personally returned the

ILG's old charter — the one issued first in 1900 over the swooping signature of Sam Gompers. The AFL convention that fall adopted a watered-down version of an ILG resolution calling for the exclusion of "all racketeering influence." Dubinsky was disappointed that its action was not stronger. That night, in a New Orleans restaurant, the little, round Dubinsky was slugged by Joey Fay, vice-president of the International Union of Operating Engineers, who was later jailed on charges of extortion. Years later, when the labor movement was compelled to take a closer look at the question of corruption, Dubinsky again came forward. As a member of the AFL-CIO Ethical Practices Committee, he welcomed the expulsion of Teamster President Dave Beck. It represented a "new cardinal principle" for organized labor, he said; the unions "are not the property of any official, no matter what his title; they belong to their members."

Dubinsky's "cardinal principle" was not "new" in the ILG. The notion that the union belonged to its members was reflected in a broad array of services and benefits that opened up or explored new vistas — both for ILG members and for the labor movement. The last bill signed by President John F. Kennedy, two days before his assassination, authorized a congressional medal commemorating the fiftieth anniversary of the nation's first union health center. That first center had opened on January 1, 1914, to carry on the ILG's tiny but insistent campaign against tuberculosis. Over the years, the Union Health Center became the point of departure for still broader programs, health and safety legislation, sickness benefits, health education. Today it is the largest link in an ILGWU chain of thirteen centers, five mobile health units, four health survey units, some medical service programs. The union continues its concern, dating from the Protocol of 1910, with standards of sanitation and safety and health in the workshop. It has developed extensive retirement schemes for its members. It has in recent years built thousands of units of housing for its own people and invested its funds in several public housing projects.

The immigrant looked to education as the lever that would raise himself and his children to a better life. The ILG's education activities reflected that hope. They started with simple lectures or musical entertainments, branched out to broad schedules of classes. In 1916, the union created its General Education Committee, and the ILG became an apostle of workers' education in the AFL. The thousands of "NRA babies" who flooded into the union, "strangers to our organization," as Dubinsky put it, provided new impetus — and a new challenge — to educational efforts. The union published countless pamphlets, booklets, labor songs, films, posters, as well as its own newspaper in several languages. It organized weekend schools and summer institutes. It founded a Labor Stage as still another means of self-expression. Out of it came *Pins and Needles,* a smash hit musical that played a "command performance" at the White House for President Roosevelt and ran for nearly five years on Broadway and on national tour. At Unity House, in the Pocono Mountains, the ILG built an elaborate vacation center, host each year to thousands of vacationing garment workers and their families.

In an industry characterized by large numbers of relatively small employers, the ILG in many ways is the unifying force. It has urged, pushed, even threatened employers to improve their work methods for their own greater profit and to make possible still better earnings for their employees. It has used its own industrial engineers,

172

its own research, its own methods to encourage efficiency and improve production. It has worked to establish the ILGWU label as the hallmark of fair working conditions.

The concerns of ILG reach far. In the 1930s, the union contributed thousands of dollars to aid the victims of oppression abroad. The ILG helped to form the Labor Chest for the Aid of Oppressed Peoples of Europe, with William Green, Matthew Woll and Dubinsky as its principal leaders. In 1944, the ILG played an important part in the formation of the AFL's Free Trade Union Committee. Its purpose was to aid the free trade union movement destroyed or driven underground by totalitarian governments. It fitted in with the AFL's long-standing concern with the welfare of unions and unionists abroad. It led to opposition to the World Federation of Trade Unions in which the unions of Communist countries played a dominant role and to support in 1949 for the new International Confederation of Free Trade Unions.

In 1911, the call to ILG members to take part in the funeral procession for the victims of the Triangle fire was published in English, Yiddish and Italian. These were the tongues of the major ethnic groups in the union, the Jews and the Italians. Later came the refugees of the Near East, then the Spanish-speaking from South and Central American states. More recently, the newcomers have been Negroes and Puerto Ricans and, in some areas, Chinese. As each wave of immigration washed over New York, spreading out across the country, it left some of its people in the garment industry. Employers fleeing the unionized metropolitan areas in search of cheap labor brought new tongues, new accents into the industry and — as they were unionized — into the union. The ILG has brought to bear a wide range of educational activities, of publication and exhortation, of placement and on-the-job techniques to the task of integrating these varied people into the union.

Life once published a flattering picture of the ILGWU under the heading, "A Great and Good Union Points the Way for American Labor Movement." Blushingly, and with generous understatement, Dubinsky commented: "That was a grand story. But we mustn't take it too seriously. After all, the ILGWU is in a consumers' and not a basic industry, and most of our people belong to minority groups. We have never kidded ourselves that we could lead the whole of American labor. The best we can do is to lead ourselves as well as we can — and thus contribute something to the rest of the labor movement."

CHAPTER ELEVEN

Philip Murray

"It was nice to
have known you, Phil"

THE BATTLE broke out early in the morning of
July 6, 1892. Iron- and steelworkers lining the bank
of the Monongahela River poured a heavy fire into
the barges carrying a force of three hundred Pinkerton
guards. For a time they caught an equally heavy return
fire, then it slowly died away. Late that afternoon, the
guards gave up. The troops came to Homestead. With
the help of troops and deputies, with a growing force of
strikebreakers, with assistance from the courts, Henry Clay
Frick put the Homestead mill back into production. By
November, the strikers had exhausted all their resources.
Many of the mechanics and laborers had stuck it out all
these months, though they were excluded from the union;
now they returned to work. The Amalgamated Association,
whose members had been Frick's target from the start,
were blacklisted. When the Amalgamated formally ended
its strike, Frick was happy; the principal owner, Andrew
Carnegie, vacationing in Italy, was jubilant. Unionism was
dead at Homestead — and in much of the steel country
around it — for years to come. Most of what was left died

in a later effort to extend unionism in the plants of the newly formed giant, United States Steel.

In 1919, "a deep, dark anger" among steelworkers burst out in a gigantic strike. Over 200,000 men turned out at the start, growing to 300,000 before many days passed. The strike grew from a broad-scale organizing campaign sponsored by the American Federation of Labor and led by William Z. Foster — a onetime syndicalist and later a prominent Communist — and John Fitzpatrick, president of the Chicago Federation of Labor. President Wilson as well as Sam Gompers made strenuous efforts to persuade the steel companies to sit down with union representatives. Judge Elbert Gary, chairman of the board of U. S. Steel, simply turned a deaf ear.

The steel companies met the strike with the full blast of their wealth and influence. It ended in utter defeat. The Interchurch World Movement Report summed up the reasons: "The United States Steel Corporation was too big . . . had too large a cash surplus, too many allies among businesses, too much support from government officers . . . Too strong influence with social institutions such as the press and the pulpit . . . too spread out over too much of the earth . . . to be defeated by widely scattered workers of many minds, many fears, varying states of pocketbook and under a comparatively improvised leadership." Company spies, welfare programs, elaborate (though essentially hollow) employee representation plans made sure unionism was not revived again for nearly twenty years.

John L. Lewis was sure steel could be organized. Michael F. Tighe, the practical but aging president of the Amalgamated Association of Iron, Steel and Tin Workers, doubted it. "You cannot fight a two-billion dollar diver-

United Steelworkers of America

PHILIP MURRAY

sified corporation," he said. Early in 1936, Lewis offered
the American Federation of Labor half a million dollars
if the Federation would raise another million to organize
steel. At least one AFL leader doubted that Lewis and
the CIO unions could raise that much money. Dan Tobin,
head of the Teamsters, commented, "There isn't a chance
in the world at this time to organize the steel workers."
Later, when William Green called for donations to the
AFL's steel organizing fund, 38 among the 110 affiliates
replied; 5 pledged a total of $8,625.

William Green went to the Amalgamated Association's
convention that summer. He promised the AFL would
wage a campaign among steelworkers in cooperation with
the association and other "interested, affected, and involved" organizations. Lewis offered a flat $500,000,
promised an industrial union. The convention replied that
the union would conduct its own campaign, though it
welcomed assistance from either source. The association
was unsatisfied by its discussions with Green; its officers
asked Lewis for a meeting. He replied bluntly: "The policy
of fluttering procrastination followed by your board is
already responsible for the loss of some weeks of time
and must be abandoned." He warned that Green would
offer only "meaningless words and further delay." If they
had not made up their minds, he suggested they stay home.
In June, 1936, the Amalgamated joined the CIO, the CIO
established the Steel Workers Organizing Committee and
put up $500,000 for a union drive in steel. To head SWOC,
Lewis chose Philip Murray, until then a relatively little-
known vice-president of the United Mine Workers.

Philip Murray, son of a miner and union man, was
born on May 25, 1886. He attended his first strike meeting
— his father was presiding — at the age of six. He himself

became a miner when he was ten. Arriving in America in 1902, father and son — his mother died when he was two — almost at once went to work in the mines around Pittsburgh. When Phil was eighteen, he slugged a check-weighman who, he was convinced, was cheating him. He was promptly fired, and six hundred miners went on strike in protest. Murray was made president of the union, and the strikers stayed out for a month. But hunger drove them back to work, and Phil was forced to leave town.

Unionism became his major interest. He was elected to the International union's executive board in 1912; four years later he became president of the union's District 5. When Lewis stepped up to the presidency, Murray became vice-president. Through all the hectic years when Lewis was building his iron-fisted control over the union, Murray worked alongside him. He differed with Lewis only on party politics. When Lewis supported Hoover, Murray went out of his way to make clear his support for Franklin Roosevelt. Murray was the man whom Lewis chose for the toughest assignment — and the highest compliment — within his reach.

Murray opened headquarters in Pittsburgh, recruited three miners' officials to head SWOC's districts. In little more than a month, SWOC had opened forty-two subdistrict offices, had begged, borrowed and stolen organizers from every source to man its drive. Business publications watched developments with respect and a little awe. "SWOC has adopted the most up-to-date and efficient business methods," observed *Iron Age,* a leading industry publication. *Fortune* commented, ". . . the SWOC's modern organizing technique . . . has adopted the suave methods of big business. This is good medicine for the workers' congenital inferiority complex." Organizers swept into steel towns along the Monongahela, into Youngstown, Aliquippa, Gary. SWOC promised steelworkers there would be no initiation fee and no dues for a year. Murray encouraged company unions to "keep biting at the heels of management." He exposed the companies' weaknesses, claiming credit for every gesture they made toward their employees. "For the first time in the history of the United States," declared *Barron's Weekly*, "industrial management is faced with a labor movement which is smart and courageous, wealthy and successful — a movement, moreover, which is winning its battle by applying a shrewd imitation of big business and organization technique."

In huge ads, the steel industry charged the SWOC was advocating "the closed shop" and interfering with economic recovery. It charged the unionists with "intimidation, coercion and violence." It vowed it would do all it could to protect steelworkers from "outsiders" butting into their industry. The industry expanded its labor spy system — "as old as the ark," *Fortune* reported, and resurrected "the equally venerable device of granting concessions (which the CIO at once claims as the by-products of its drive)." The companies instituted time-and-a-half pay for work after forty-eight hours — though few steelworkers worked more than forty-eight — one-week vacations and occasional pay raises. The industry built up its stores of tear gas, gas masks and riot guns. But nothing stemmed the flood of steelworkers into the union. Company unions joined in bodies. By January, 1937, SWOC claimed some 125,000 members. At the moment, the nation was intent on the auto workers' battle with General Motors, and the sit-down strike at Flint. John L. Lewis, leaving New York for embattled Detroit, told reporters, "Let there be no moaning at the bar when I put out to sea." But Lewis had already held his first talks with Myron C. Taylor, the head of U. S. Steel. They were resumed once Lewis settled the General Motors strike. On March 2, standing under a picture of a once-jubilant Andrew Carnegie at the Carnegie-Illinois plant, Murray signed an agreement with Benjamin Fairless, president of Carnegie-Illinois, U. S. Steel's principal subsidiary. With that document, U. S. Steel, the giant and leader of the nation's most basic industry, recognized SWOC as the representative of its members, established a minimum wage of 62½ cents an hour, a forty-hour week with time-and-a-half overtime, one week's vacation, seniority, a grievance procedure. Coupled with the CIO victories in autos, the Big Steel agreement gave fresh impetus to union membership. That summer, too, the Supreme Court validated the Wagner Act. Passed in 1935 after the death of NRA, the Wagner Act wrote into law the substance of Section 7(a) — the right to join a union and to bargain collectively. Industry scoffed at the law until the Supreme Court in 1937 gave it teeth. Company after company came under union contract. In steel, SWOC doubled its membership by the end of the summer.

Four companies refused to budge — the four known as Little Steel. Ads of the Iron and Steel Institute sought to discredit SWOC and the CIO. The companies stockpiled industrial munitions — $178,000 worth, according to the La Follette Committee — and hired more guards. On May 25, SWOC struck twenty-seven plants of Republic Steel, Youngstown Sheet and Tube, Inland Steel and, soon after, Bethlehem Steel. On Memorial Day, in an open field fronting the South Chicago mills of Republic Steel, strikers and sympathizers faced a long line of police. Somebody in the crowd, one reporter noted, threw a branch skyward. A

181

policeman fired his revolver at it. "For one brief instant of time there was confusion: a rumble; a loud, weird rumble of noise" as police opened fire. Forty in the crowd were wounded; ten died, all hit from behind. The outburst of brutality, the La Follette Committee said, "has seldom been equaled in the savage industrial conflicts of the past." Armed deputies cleared the way for food deliveries to strike-breakers. Special police reopened the Republic plant. Citizens' committees fostered back-to-work movements. Mediators, state and federal, could find no basis for settlement in the face of Little Steel's stubborn stand. In the end, the men returned to work with virtually no gains to show for their efforts.

The loss was not fatal. SWOC pursued the companies before the National Labor Relations Board and in the courts. There, Little Steel was compelled to recognize and deal with the union. The depression of 1937 slowed the union even more. More than a quarter of its membership was thrown out of work; many more thousands were cut back to a day or two a week. Employers, with their production down to about a fifth of capacity, pressed for wage cuts. Murray was able, though, to negotiate a "standstill" agreement that renewed existing wage scales without change. As both production and employment increased, the union renewed its advance.

The war in Europe imposed a heavy — and growing — burden on Murray's friendship with Lewis. Increasingly, Murray found himself at odds over foreign policy with his longtime associate. Murray refused to withhold his support from Roosevelt, as Lewis publicly vowed he would. When Lewis was faced with fulfilling his promise to resign, Phil Murray was prominently and frequently mentioned as his logical successor. Murray denied any desire to replace

Lewis; he insisted he had only respect and admiration and affection for him. Sidney Hillman, though, derailed the keep-Lewis bandwagon and Lewis stepped down — in part, perhaps, because he felt Murray was still his lieutenant, that through him he would retain a decisive voice in the CIO. Lewis nominated Murray for the post, and he was elected.

Lewis retained a number of his alliances in the CIO for a time. Many union leaders, steel and clothing workers excepted, continued to look to Lewis for advice. In the fall of 1941, Lewis and Murray met during the CIO convention at Atlantic City. Lewis still urged opposition to President Roosevelt's foreign policy; Murray insisted with equal strength on its full support. They attempted to talk it out during a walk on the famed boardwalk, but their strong disagreement ended in a thick silence. For a while they walked, then Lewis held out his hand. "It was nice to have known you, Phil."

The rupture of their lifetime association was confirmed soon after the first of the year. Without warning or consultation, Lewis called on both Green and Murray for what he called "an accouplement" of the AFL and CIO. A *New York Times* article claimed that Lewis and several AFL leaders had already agreed on how it would be done. Green would step aside, George Meany would become president and Murray secretary-treasurer of the united labor movement. Lewis would have a place on its executive council. Murray learned about it for the first time on a train returning from a vacation. He exploded: "No one has the right to trade me for a job. Jobs are not sufficiently alluring where principles are concerned." He accused Lewis of "Pearl Harbor-ing" him. More formally, he advised Lewis that he would take up the proposal with the executive board of the CIO. Lewis claimed he was acting as head of a labor peace committee formed in 1939 and never dissolved. But President Roosevelt apparently was not anxious to see Lewis returned to power, even indirectly. He proposed a joint wartime labor advisory board. The two groups quickly accepted, and Lewis' proposed "accouplement" was forgotten. Later that year, Lewis stopped the Miners' dues payments to the CIO. He had his "former friend" hailed before a Miners' policy committee. There he was lashed with angry accusations in a grueling trial. Then, despite the lengthy trial and acting on his own, Lewis ruled that Murray was ineligible to continue as vice-president of the United Mine Workers. He had accepted, Lewis pointed out, the presidency of the newly formed United Steelworkers of America.

Murray led the new union — the successor to SWOC — to a series of new wage agreements that boosted steelworkers' wages and improved their working conditions. In 1949, the Steelworkers raised the issue of an employer-paid pension. The idea, Big Steel's Benjamin Fairless said, was a "revolutionary doctrine." Murray questioned the double standard by which executives received huge company-paid pensions but workers paid in part for their own. On October 1, the Steelworkers struck. By the end of the month, Bethlehem agreed to a $100-a-month pension (at age sixty-five after working twenty-five years). Shortly, U. S. Steel granted a similar pension. By the end of the month the industry was back at work and the Steelworkers' pension a fact.

When Sidney Hillman died, Murray named Jack Kroll, also from the Clothing Workers, to head the CIO Political Action Committee. The announcement that Vice-President Henry A. Wallace — the CIO's first choice in 1944

— would run for the presidency in 1948 on the Progressive Party ticket brought a quick response from Kroll. The CIO, he said, had never supported a third party. His stand was backed — 33 to 11 — by the CIO executive board and President Truman endorsed for reelection. "The issue split the organization," says historian Philip Taft, "and was the forerunner of action against the Communists."

The Communist Party, by then, had been active in the labor movement for some three decades. It had fostered the Trade Union Education League in the early 1920s in an effort to organize its own factions inside the unions. In 1928 it switched to the Trade Union Unity League, which attempted to organize separate and dual unions. It managed to create several — the Needle Trades Industrial Union was one — but they were neither successful nor important. In the midthirties, the Communist tactics changed again. They returned to the old practice of "boring from within" — of seeking to gain power within already established unions or at least to create coalitions in which they had a voice.

In 1936, Lewis said: "I am for labor and I will go with anyone who will work with me in this cause." Liberals and radicals of every hue flocked to the CIO colors. Lewis welcomed back men he had driven from his own union and had accused of disruptive influences. Among the hundreds who worked on the CIO and CIO union payrolls were a goodly number of Communists, alleged Communists, Socialists, radicals of every viewpoint. "It is a pretty good rule," Lewis said, "to work with anyone who will work with you." The left wing supported Lewis in his stand against Roosevelt's foreign policy. Some left Lewis in the presidential contest of 1940. More abandoned him when the Nazi armies invaded the Soviet Union in

the summer of 1941 and the Communist attitude toward
the war in Europe reversed directions. Soon Lewis stood
alone. Excepting only the Miners, the CIO solidly supported
the Roosevelt foreign policy backed by Murray. But sharp
differences were renewed, soon after the end of the war,
over the Marshall Plan for aiding war-torn European
countries. Murray was not yet ready for an all-out assault
on the CIO left wing, but he did bring Secretary of State
George C. Marshall to the 1947 convention to defend the
Marshall Plan and the Truman foreign policies. The differences were sharpened when Murray and most of the CIO
leaders backed Truman, while the left wing supported
Wallace. Murray dismissed some staff members, removed
a number of officials from CIO office for their failure to
accept the CIO back-Truman policy. At the 1948 convention, he accused the left of subverting "every decent movement into which they may have affiliated themselves in
the course of their unholy career." He took the CIO out
of the World Federation of Trade Unions that Hillman
had labored to build.

At the 1949 convention, the resolutions committee
headed by Walter Reuther, president of the United Auto
Workers, accused the left-wingers of acting as puppets of
the Soviet Union. Harry Bridges, head of the West Coast
longshoremen's union, replied, "The real issue is they don't
want opposition. You can vote, but when you do make
sure you vote right." It meant, he insisted, that the opposition was being told to get in line with the executive board
or get booted out. The longshoremen, he maintained, had
a right to follow their own policies. But the convention
booted out two unions — the United Electrical, Radio and
Machine Workers and the tiny Farm Equipment Workers.
A convention resolution declared "we can no longer tolerate

within the family of the CIO the Communist Party masquerading as a labor union." It accused the UE of acting as a "labor base" for the party, "an echo of the Comintern." The convention barred any member of the Communist Party from serving on the executive board. And it authorized the executive board to take action against ten other unions. Charges were filed against them a few weeks later and a trial committee appointed to hear them. But the accused unions refused to appear. The committee nevertheless recommended the expulsion of nine, and the executive board complied. Several of the ousted unions quickly collapsed. The CIO chartered a new union of Electrical, Radio and Machine Workers, which won over a majority of the ousted UE. The longshoremen and mill, mine and smelter workers continued as independent unions.

In December, 1952, Philip Murray died. Thirteen days later, death took William Green. Once more the trade union movement changed course.

CHAPTER TWELVE

Walter Reuther

"The most dangerous man in Detroit"

JACOB REUTHER left his dairy farm at Mannheim, Germany, and came to America to keep his sons out of the Kaiser's army and to stave off persecution for his political ideas. One of his sons, Valentine, became a brewery worker, a Socialist and a vigorous unionist. Valentine was, according to one of his own sons, "an old soapboxer, an old rabble-rouser who indoctrinated his boys when they were pretty young, and he told them the thing most important in the world to fight for was the other guy, the brotherhood of man, the Golden rule . . . an old fighter in the ranks of labor, a trade-unionist from away back when the going was rough."

Valentine earned $1.50 a day at the Schmulbach Brewery in Wheeling, West Virginia. In his spare time, he ran the local brewery workers' union, and he was chosen, when just twenty-three, to head the Ohio Valley Trades and Labor Assembly. An ardent admirer of Gene Debs, Valentine once ran for Congress on the Socialist ticket. When Debs was imprisoned for a short time at nearby Moundsville Prison, he took his sons to meet the

famous man. His son Walter was born in 1907, educated
in part at Ritchie Grammar School and Wheeling High.
He delivered newspapers, organized a championship basket-
ball team, shared in the union's family picnics and its
socials at the union hall. Another and important part
of his education came from his father's Sunday-after-
church debates. Each week, Valentine assigned Walter and
his brothers a topic; they boned up on it at the local
library. Sunday afternoons, with Valentine as chairman,
they debated the question. Trade unions, politics and
economics always had a prominent place in the discussions.

Walter left school at sixteen to become a toolmaker's
apprentice. He started at Wheeling Steel, where his older
brother Ted worked. He was fired for organizing a protest
against working on Sunday, and went to Detroit, where
he was later joined by his younger brothers Victor and
Roy. Walter got a job on the night shift at the Briggs
body plant at 85 cents an hour. Later he talked himself
into a tool-and-die-maker's job at Ford at $1.10 an hour.
At the same time, he went back to school, finishing high
school and starting on social sciences at Wayne University.
He worked at Ford from 3:30 P.M. to midnight, studied
several hours, and still turned up for an eight o'clock class
in sociology. He organized a club to discuss social problems, campaigned against bringing R.O.T.C. to the campus,
stumped for Norman Thomas, the frequent Socialist candidate for President, in the 1932 elections. In 1933, owing
partly to his strong interest in a union for auto workers,
he was fired.

Jobs were scarce in 1933. With a few hundred dollars
in savings, Walter and Victor set off on a world tour.
They bicycled thousands of miles, slept in hostels or
haystacks, and worked when they went broke. They visited

189

United Auto Workers

WALTER REUTHER

auto plants and textile mills in Britain. They saw the smoking ruins of the Reichstag in Berlin; while visiting their mother's home town, they saw Nazi students beat up a young worker. In the Soviet Union, their Detroit skills won them jobs in the Gorki auto plant. Walter became a crew leader, teaching young Russian workers to use close-fitting, American-type techniques. When Roy wrote that the union situation in Detroit was bubbling up, they returned home.

Unionism had never been able to gain a hold in the auto industry. By converting production to an assembly line in the early years of the century, Henry Ford drained much of the skill from the jobs and put them within reach of vast numbers of lower-skilled workers. In mid-winter, 1914, Henry Ford announced an unheard-of $5-a-day wage. Thousands lined up at the employment office and riots broke out among the disappointed jobseekers. Police quelled the brawling with fire hoses despite the icy weather. Although the worker had to stay on the job six months to get the $5-a-day pay, it cut down on job turn-over, and gave Ford the pick of the available men. Ford called it "one of the finest cost-cutting moves we ever made."

The assembly line demanded no high skill or lengthy training. Instead, it demanded continuous, intense, repeti-tious work, sustained constantly by the endlessly moving line. The pressure mounted as the line was speeded up and men changed jobs often in an effort to avoid its unceasing push. Seasonal layoffs and model change-overs left the workers stranded without income of any kind. But auto plants became the goals of thousands, white and black, who migrated to Detroit in search for work.

A union of auto workers was formed in 1913, but it

made little headway. The AFL attempted to recruit auto workers in the mid-1920s — skilled workers and maintenance crafts in craft unions, production workers in federal locals. But it never really got started. The depression cut jobs in the auto plants from nearly half a million to half that — and many of those worked part time. Over 200,000 were on Detroit's relief rolls in 1931, and 150,000 went back home. One latter-day union member recalled being taken to a plant window by his foreman who pointed "to all those guys standing outside the employment gate. 'If you don't like your job there's plenty of them outside who want it.'"

Soon after the National Recovery Act was passed, AFL organizers moved into Detroit; auto workers themselves began organizing. President Roosevelt set up the Auto Labor Board in an effort to stem the tide of discontent, unrest, strike threats and strike calls that boiled up in the plants. The board's failure to act and finally its recognition of company-dominated employee representation plans destroyed any usefulness it might have had. Sidney Hillman paved the way for an NRA investigation of the industry. Leon Henderson, who conducted the probe, reported: "Labor unrest exists to a degree higher than warranted by the depression. The unrest flows from insecurity, low annual earnings, inequitable hiring and rehiring methods, espionage, speedup, and displacement of workers at an extremely early age. . . . Unless something is done soon, [the workers] intend to take things into their own hands to get results." The Henderson report found the auto plants hiring only the younger men, those least friendly to the union and men of forty who had trouble finding jobs or being rehired after layoffs. It found General Motors paying the Pinkerton Corporation $419,000 and the Chrysler

Corporation paying Corporation Auxiliaries Corporation $211,000 for labor spy and guard services.

In ,February, 1935, William Green proposed an international union of auto workers. The Machinists claimed that "setup men" belonged to them. Green objected: "They are mass-minded. They ask me over and over again. Are you going to divide us up? I cannot change that state of mind; it is there. We cannot organize them on any other basis." Over Lewis' and Dubinsky's objections, the executive council voted to exclude tool-and-die makers and machinery maintenance men from the auto workers' charter. Green promised to try to carry out the council's decision, but, he said, "I know we will fail." The auto workers objected to being divided up; they objected to Green naming the officers of their union. In April, 1936, at a convention at South Bend, they declared their independence. A month later, they joined the CIO.

On his return from his travels, Walter Reuther went to work at the Ternstedt plant of General Motors, only to be fired for his union activities. He was a delegate to the South Bend convention — though it took his local's last five dollars to get him there — and was elected to the national executive board. He set up shop as a volunteer organizer, merged a number of small locals into one, with a membership of seventy-eight. To organize one plant — the Kelsey-Hayes Wheel Corporation — he borrowed the stay-in tactics used by rubber workers at Akron and Bendix workers at South Bend. He arranged for a girl to faint at the assembly line. That was the signal for key union members to pull the switches and stop work. A bewildered personnel director agreed to call in Reuther to get the people back to work. Instead, Reuther mounted a box and launched into an organizing speech, while fellow unionists handed out application blanks. When the personnel director objected, Reuther explained, "I can't put them back to work until I get them organized." Success at Kelsey-Hayes brought auto workers clambering to get into the union. "A guy we never heard of," Reuther recalled, "would call up and say, 'We've shut down such-and-such plant. Send us over some coffee and doughnuts.' So we'd send over the stuff. Later on, we organized central kitchens and mobile feeding units. . . . We slept hardly at all. That's how we grew."

The union swept through the auto plants, winning a tense and decisive climax in the General Motors sitdown strikes. Victory at General Motors was followed by strikes — and similar agreements — at Chrysler, Packard, Studebaker. The sitdown strikes were widely and emphatically denounced — as conspiracies against property rights, as illegal seizures, as sheer revolution. But the sitdowns had advantages for the strikers: no picket lines, less chance for clashes with police, less chance for strikebreakers to take their jobs. A 1937 convention resolution declared: "The stay-in strike was beyond a doubt the only method by which the workers in the automobile industry could have forced the employers, who were determined to disregard the law of the land, into entering into a real collective bargaining relationship — and without loss of life." In 1939, the U. S. Supreme Court found the sitdowns unlawful. By then, though, much — perhaps most — of their purpose had been accomplished.

Success brought its problems. A sharp division arose in the union, and factions formed to seek control. The depression of 1937 faced the union with problems of reduced income and the necessity of cutting its staff. To preserve peace and some measure of unity in the union, the CIO sent in teams of union leaders: John L. Lewis and David Dubinsky in 1937, Philip Murray and Sidney Hillman in 1938. Their efforts blew up when Homer Martin, the former minister turned union president, suspended a number of national executive board members. In turn, he was impeached. Martin called a convention in Detroit in competition with a special union convention in Cleveland. The latter clearly held the loyalty of most auto workers. Martin and his small handful joined the AFL.

General Motors attempted to use the apparently contradictory claims of the two groups to suspend collective bargaining. Reuther, then head of the United Auto Workers' GM department, came up with the "strategy strike" as the answer to GM's "convenient confusion." He called out the key tool-and-die makers at the moment the company was changing models. Without them, the work slowed down, then came to a halt. The nonstriking workers were laid off and were able to claim unemployment insurance benefits. The UAW won exclusive bargaining rights throughout most of the corporation's plants.

Only Ford among the principal auto makers remained. A former sailor and prizefighter by the name of Harry Bennett was in charge of labor relations at Ford. He commanded an ugly crew of fighters and wrestlers and former convicts that he used, like storm troopers, to keep the workers under the Ford thumb. Union organizers, launching a drive in 1937, were met outside the plant gates in what came to be called the "battle of the overpass." Bennett's "servicemen" set on Reuther, Richard Frankensteen and other UAW organizers, brutally beat and kicked them down the stairs. Reuther later testified: "They picked me up about eight different times and threw me down on my back on the concrete . . . they kicked me in the face, hands, and other parts of my body. . . . After they kicked me down all the stairs then they started to hit me at the bottom of the stairs, hit me and slugged me, driving me before them, but never letting me get away."

Now that the Supreme Court had upheld the Wagner Act, the UAW filed charges with the National Labor Relations Board. Ford replied with terror, labor spies, firings. Between 1936 and 1941, thousands were discharged for union activities. The board ordered Ford to bargain with the union; the company ignored the order. The Circuit Court of Appeals affirmed the order, and the Supreme Court refused to review it. Posters went up in the plants declaring the right of the men to join the union; then Bennett fired eight more union members. The men just quit working, the strike spreading from shop to shop until the company's massive River Rouge plant stood idle. A formal strike was called that midnight. All through that night, the Ford strikers talked. Feeling the texture of freedom, the discussion went on, it seemed, almost endlessly. Emil Mazey, later secretary of the union, remembered the amazing all-night meeting: "It was like seeing men who had been half-dead come to life. . . . It was hard to keep things going, hard to organize, so eager were they just to mill around and talk and let some steam go." To counter the brawn of Bennett's servicemen, the UAW organized barricades of autos. They crowded all the incoming roads, even the drawbridges leading to the Ford Works, until it was almost impossible to get in or out. The strike ended April 10, and in May the National Labor Relations Board conducted an election among some 80,000 Ford workers. Over 58,000 cast their votes for the UAW. Then, in a sharp and surprising about-face, Bennett signed

196

an agreement that gave the union a full union shop and a checkoff of union dues. It established seniority, grievance machinery, time-and-a-half for overtime, premium pay for night work. The company was also compelled to reinstate 2,566 workers it had fired during its fight against the UAW and pay them two million dollars in back wages.

Once, after a heated bargaining session, William Knudsen, GM's vigorous production chief, told Reuther, "Young man, I wish you were selling used cars for us." "Used cars?" Reuther echoed. "Sure," Knudsen replied, "anybody can sell new cars." Another observer described the impression Reuther conveys — and "fosters": ". . . mind always working, tongue clacking furiously, ideas spinning out in endless reel." George Romney, the auto maker who became governor of Michigan, called him "the most dangerous man in Detroit because no one is more skillful in bringing about the revolution without seeming to disturb the existing forms of society."

In 1940, Reuther startled the country with a proposal to build an incredible five hundred airplanes a day. He was quickly denounced as almost everything from a revolutionary to a crackpot. In essence, he proposed that the government draft idle auto plants, tools and machines in much the same way it was drafting men for the armed services. Use the new tools, jigs, and fixtures intended for the 1942 model cars to supplement existing basic machinery. Finally, give labor a share, along with government and management, in directing the operation. The proposal was quickly "brushed-off." Secretary of the Treasury Morgenthau commented: "There is only one thing wrong with the program. It comes from the 'wrong' source." In fact, when auto production was finally canceled to make

way for war production, some elements of Reuther's plan
were adopted. The industry eventually used more auto tools
than they had admitted in 1940 was possible.

The five-hundred-planes-a-day proposal was only the
first of a number of Reuther "plans." His proposals for
standardizing tank engine production were adopted. He
suggested soldiers and workers could understand each
other's problems better if they put soldiers in the plants
and workers in the training camps; it was adopted. He
had a plan for raising the sunken liner *Normandie,* which
was rejected. Several other Reuther plans cropped up in
the years ahead.

The union adopted a "no strike" pledge for the duration
of World War II, but linked it with an "equality of sacri-
fice" program. It fought for rationing of scarce consumer
goods, such as food, clothing, housing. It urged wage increases to meet rising prices, security allowances for
dependents of servicemen, payment of overtime in non-
negotiable war bonds — to be cashed after the war ended.
The Communist-led bloc in the union sponsored a proposal
to bring back piecework and incentive pay to increase
production in the war plants. Earl Browder, the Communist
leader, called it "patriotic." The Reuther forces called it
speedup — more work without correspondingly more pay.
Reuther led the fight that defeated it in the 1943 convention. As the end of the war approached — and as it became
clear that Reuther was aiming for the UAW presidency —
factions crystallized. Reuther was able to enlist the support
of a good many secondary leaders — shop committeemen,
stewards, local officers, along with a good many Socialists,
conservatives, Southerners, Catholics and others who were
dissatisfied with the union's leaders. President R. J. Thomas
and Secretary-Treasurer George F. Addes were the center

198

of a bloc with strong Communist Party participation, but with a non-Communist following as well. Reuther focused his attack on the Communist core. He did not object to the Communist group because it represented a political party, good, bad, or indifferent, he said; he opposed it because it was the willing agent of a totalitarian power. He pounded away at the idea that it was neither a native nor a legitimate party of discontent. The two factions refought the battle of piecework and incentive pay. And they fought over Reuther's strategy in his most recent battle with General Motors.

Soon after VJ Day, Reuther asked General Motors for a startling 30 per cent wage increase. He claimed GM could pay the increase without raising its prices and still make more profit than it had before the war. Moreover, it was in line with President Truman's policy of allowing wage increases that did not call for price boosts. GM offered 10 per cent — if it could get government approval to raise the prices of its cars. Reuther demanded GM open its books to get at the facts. GM indignantly refused, called his demand an unwarranted interference with "management prerogatives." On November 21, some two hundred thousand GM workers walked out in a strike that lasted 113 days. The way to a settlement was finally opened when a presidential fact-finding commission recommended a 19½-cents-an-hour increase. The auto workers promptly accepted; GM just as promptly refused. Then, the United Electrical Workers settled their contract for 18½ cents an hour, followed by the Steelworkers. The UAW was forced to settle for the same amount.

The Thomas-Addes faction accused Reuther of unnecessarily sacrificing the GM workers. It sneered at Reuther's "fancy economics." Philip Murray came to the 1946 UAW convention and let it be known that he favored Thomas over Reuther. "I have a soft spot in my heart for the big fellow," he said. Reuther won the presidency, though, in a close race, but his opponents won control of the national executive board and reelected Addes. The Reuther group intensified its efforts. It carried its campaign into countless union halls and local meetings. In 1947, Reuther scored close to a clean sweep. His group elected its candidates to the two vice-presidencies, twenty of the twenty-four seats on the national executive board and replaced Addes with Emil Mazey. At the convention's end, Reuther summed it up: "If the editorial writers . . . are inclined to write that the UAW and the leadership in this convention are drifting toward a more conservative policy, I say . . . they are wrong, because this convention and its leadership is committed to the kind of militant, fighting trade-union program that will mobilize not only our union but the people in America in support of an aggressive over-all economic, social, and political program." He added: "We are the vanguard in America in the great crusade to build a better world. We are the architects of the future."

In the CIO, Reuther continued the fight against the Communist left that he had started in his campaign for the UAW presidency. He opposed the supporters of Wallace for President. In the 1948 CIO convention he charged that "colonial agents of a foreign government are using the trade unions as an operating base." He demanded they "get clear in the CIO or clear out." He contended that if the left wing used its democratic rights to urge its policies and oppose others, it was obligated to accept the majority decision. He joined with Murray in 1949 in ousting the Electrical Workers and the Farm Equipment

Workers and in paving the way for the expulsion of nine others.

Reuther once commented that if leading a union meant no more than winning six cents an hour for its members, he was not interested. A union, he repeatedly made clear, has a broader role to play. "We've got to be a constructive social force working to advance the welfare of the whole community." His goal, he told another, is not to patch up the world so that "men can starve less often . . . but a labor movement that will remake the world so that working people will get the benefit of their labor." And he said, in another connection, "We shall hold on to our gains only by making progress with the community — not at the expense of the community."

As president of the UAW he has led a restless search for ways of making his union more effective. "A labor movement can get soft and flabby spiritually," he told a recent union convention. "It can make progress materially and the soul of the union can die in the process." When a depression threatened in 1949, he proposed the use of idle aircraft plants to produce twenty million low-priced prefabricated houses. Again, some people snorted, but his proposal underscored an urgent national need. He led the Auto Workers to pensions and to broad health care programs.

In 1961 he negotiated a profit-sharing agreement with American Motors — an area where unions had almost always feared, or refused, to tread. For too long, profit-sharing had been an employer sop to underpaid workers.

In 1957, the Auto Workers established a Public Review Board. To it any member could bring a grievance or complaint against the union. The board was given, *New York*

Times reporter A. H. Raskin commented, "the broadest grant of authority over its internal affairs ever given voluntarily by a labor body — or any other organization — to an outside body." The UAW opened a leadership school, intending to introduce its paid officials to everything from "labor morality to the language of computers." Reuther told the first class: "If you go back home and do everything the way you did before, this school will be a failure." Raskin also reported a week-long session of the union's executive board devoted to a discussion of long-range problems — to answering the question, where is the union going? Said one board member: "We're getting older. You can't keep talking to a guy about what happened in the depression when he wasn't even born."

In December, 1952, Philip Murray died. Walter Reuther became the third — and last — president of the Congress of Industrial Organizations.

CHAPTER THIRTEEN

George Meany

"A plumber who paints like Grandma Moses"

I N THAT SAME December of 1952, William Green died. The executive council promptly chose George Meany as his successor, the fourth — and last — president of the American Federation of Labor. A onetime plumber, a longtime union official, Meany stood about five feet ten, weighed in at well over two hundred pounds packed on a thick, heavyset frame — the perfect setting for a gruff, direct, blunt personality. Associates described him as a tough, fierce competitor who played gin rummy with intense concentration, a better-than-average golfer until a rheumatic hip forced him onto canes. In exuberant moods, he sometimes pounded out ditties on a piano or broke into song in a strong, pleasant baritone. He enjoyed painting — *Business Week* dubbed him "a plumber who paints like Grandma Moses."

George Meany was born August 16, 1894, at 125th Street and Madison Avenue in New York City's Harlem. He was brought up in the Port Morris section of the Bronx, one of ten children of Anna and Michael Meany. His father was a foreman plumber and president of Local 2. On Sundays, Meany recalled, a steady stream of visitors flowed through the Meany house. "I can remember those men talking about something known as 'the organization' and I may say to you that they did not pronounce it that way. They called it the 'organ-eye-zation.' But I can remember the reverence in which they used the term and inculcated into my mind at that time was the thought that whatever the organization was, it was something with these men almost on a par with religion. I grew up with faith in the trade-union movement."

He left school after his first year in high school. He worked briefly as a messenger boy for an advertising agency. At sixteen, he became an apprentice plumber; at nineteen, a journeyman. Sunday, he played catcher on a semipro baseball team. At other times, he took in the fights at Madison Square Garden or took his girl, Eugenia McMahon, to a dance. Sometimes he walked a picket line with her when her union — the International Ladies Garment Workers — called a strike. They were married in 1919.

He was elected to the executive board of his local union in 1920, and in 1922 — when he was twenty-eight — he became a business agent. A friend of those days described him as "an everything-on-the-level kind of guy." In 1923, he was elected secretary-treasurer of the New York Building Trades Council. He took a 50 per cent cut in pay during the depression years; at one point, he went without salary for nine months. In 1934 he became president of the New York State Federation of Labor.

His main job as head of the state federation was to "lobby" labor's legislative program through the state legislature. He had over a hundred bills ready for the 1935 session. When it ended, he could point to seventy-two

Fabian Bachrach for AFL-CIO

GEORGE MEANY

laws. *Time* said the New York legislature passed more labor bills during Meany's time as labor's lobbyist "than it had ever enacted before or has since." Meany fought to establish prevailing pay on WPA projects. He insisted that a man working on a work relief project was entitled to the same rate of pay as a man doing the same work for a private employer. A series of strikes and Meany's persistence settled the question in his favor. He opposed Tammany Hall, the "regular" Democratic organization, to win union support for Fiorello La Guardia as mayor of New York. He would have nothing to do with the American Labor Party, the Lewis-Hillman-Dubinsky group in New York. He dismissed it as "political self-seekers, left-wingers, political renegades and non-laboring laborites." In 1939, when Frank Morrison, the longtime secretary-treasurer of the AFL, died, Meany was chosen to succeed him. He capped his New York career with a mammoth Labor Day parade up Fifth Avenue. Ninety thousand union members and 178 bands paraded for hours — with flashlights and flares lighting the way before it ended.

In Washington, Meany was overshadowed at first by Green and the veteran presidents of powerful international unions. But he carved out a place for himself. He served effectively on the War Labor Board. He became increasingly active in international labor affairs — some said because Bill Green was not interested. In 1945, he opposed AFL participation in the World Federation of Trade Unions. Four years later, he joined in forming the International Confederation of Free Trade Unions. Under Meany the AFL — and the AFL-CIO — has played a growing role in international labor affairs.

When World War II ended, President Truman lifted the wartime lid on wage increases — first partially, then totally. Almost from VJ Day, an unequaled wave of strikes swept across the country. In 1946, there were nearly 5,000 strikes, involving some 4,600,000 workers, lasting 116,000,000 man-days. Major strikes hit the auto plants, farm implements, coal, railroads, electrical manufacturing, steel, meat-packing, oil refining, longshoremen — and countless more. No period in the nation's history could match it.

President Truman asked the 80th Congress to enact laws dealing with jurisdictional strikes and certain kinds of secondary boycotts. He suggested it consider more effective ways of avoiding strikes and lockouts. The Republican Congress — the first in decades — embarked on a vendetta against organized labor. The House Committee on Education and Labor, with scarcely a witness friendly to labor, reported that the Wagner Act and the National Labor Relations Board — "labor laws ill-conceived and disastrously executed" — had deprived the American workingman of his "dignity." He had been "cajoled, coerced, intimidated, and on many occasions beaten up, in the name of the splendid aims" of the Wagner Act. He had been, the committee declared, "subjected to tyranny more despotic than any one could think possible in a free country." A minority report warned that the majority's proposals would not "merely wipe out labor's gains under the beneficent administration of President Roosevelt; it turns the clock of history back at least a century and a half and eliminates safeguards and protections which both Republican and Democratic Congresses have sponsored for generations." The House passed the tough committee bill. A similar measure, though not quite as sweeping, passed the Senate. The two bills went to conference. Under the threat of a presidential veto, many of the worst features of the House bill were eliminated and some restrictions eased. The conference bill — the Taft-Hartley Act — was passed, but President Truman refused to sign it. He sent it back to Congress, arguing that it had been too greatly influenced by the troubles of the postwar reconversion period. He contended it would lead to more — not less — government intervention in labor relations and business. He said it was unworkable, unfair, discriminatory. Organized labor called it a "slave labor" bill, charged it would destroy the right of workers to organize and bargain collectively. Congress paid little heed to Truman or the unions. Both houses overrode the veto.

The Taft-Hartley Act extended the idea of "coercion and intimidation" to unions; until then, the Wagner Act had applied it largely to employers. Taft-Hartley outlawed the closed shop, permitted a union shop only after a majority of workers had ratified it in a government-conducted election. (This requirement was soon repealed when more than nine out of ten workers voted for the union shop in election after election; they soon were shown to be a waste of time.) It opened the door for employers to sue unions for damages. It outlawed certain union practices and subjected jurisdictional disputes and some kinds of boycotts to control by court injunction. It required officers of unions to swear that they were not members of the Communist Party or of organizations supporting it. A union whose officers failed to file these non-Communist affidavits was denied the protection of the National Labor Relations Board. It provided for injunctions that would prohibit workers from striking in so-called "national emergency" disputes during a "cooling-off" period of eighty days.

A "fighting mad" Bill Green came to the AFL convention in 1947, vowing to defeat every member of Congress who had voted for the Taft-Hartley Act. At the same time, the convention faced the immediate question of complying with the non-Communist provisions of the hated law. The executive council proposed a series of constitutional changes that would allow the Federation president and secretary-treasurer to sign the affidavits. This would clear the way for federal (directly-chartered) unions, if they saw fit, to utilize the NLRB. It would not, however, interfere with any policy that any international union adopted to comply — or to refuse to comply — with the act.

John L. Lewis (the Miners had returned to the AFL in 1946) opposed the executive council and the amendments in a sneering, arrogant, scathing speech. " 'Thou shalt not muzzle the ox that treadeth out the corn.' " Lewis began. "So runs the Scripture. But the Congress of the United States designated fifteen million workers in this country . . . as being cattle that treadeth out the economic corn of our country, and the Congress placed an economic muzzle on each of you. What are you going to do about it? Oh, I see. You are going to change the Constitution. God help us!"

He ridiculed the Federation leadership. He pictured eight million union members "trying to advance across the plains of America, led and flanked, and having their thinking done for them by intellectually fat and stately asses." He reminded the delegates that, once before, the Miners had urged a policy on the Federation. It had been ignored — to the Federation's cost. Ignore the Miners again, he predicted, and the Federation would regret it. He promised to resign his vice-presidency if the amendments were adopted; he denied he was holding a pistol to the head of the convention. "I don't think the Federation has a head. I think its neck has just grown up and haired over."

The decisive answer to Lewis' angry charge came from George Meany. He didn't think the practical problem that faced the convention could be solved "by impugning the integrity of men who feel that they can best represent their membership by complying with the law of the land." The amendments simply gave the federal unions the same option that every other union enjoyed. It left the other unions free to take whatever stand their organization felt necessary. Nor was it wise, Meany thought, to use the federal locals as "shock troops" to fight the Taft-Hartley law. "They are in no position to do so, even if the delegates wanted them to," he stated, for they had neither the backing, the experience, nor the financial standing to make the fight. Meany noted that Lewis had said that Phil Murray was the prisoner of the Communists. "I agree," Meany said. "Who walked out and left him prisoner?" As president of the Mine Workers, Meany went on, Lewis with his right hand upheld his own union's stand against Communism. With his left, he made "fellowship" with "the stinking America haters who love Moscow." Meany added: "So I am prepared to sign a non-Communist affidavit. I am prepared to go further and sign an affidavit that I never was a comrade to the comrades." The delegates approved the amendments.

A few weeks later, using a blue crayon on a half-torn, rumpled sheet of paper, Lewis wrote: "Green. We disaffiliate. Lewis." Largely as a result of the passage of the Taft-Hartley Act, the AFL launched Labor's League for Political Education. It was not so much a new design for political action, Meany said, "but an attempt to give effect to [the AFL's old political] philosophy in line with present conditions." Through the league, the AFL set out to make

its members "politically conscious, [to] develop them politically in their own self-interest."

When Meany was named to succeed Green, he moved
quickly to establish his leadership. The Teamsters' Dan
Tobin challenged his choice of William F. Schnitzler of
the Bakery Workers as secretary-treasurer. Meany promptly
put it to the executive council and was upheld, 7-6. A
few months later, William L. Hutcheson, head of the powerful Carpenters' union and first vice-president of the Federation, questioned a Meany policy on jurisdiction. He
threatened to pull his union out of the AFL to back up his
stand. Meany accepted his withdrawal before Hutcheson
had a chance to change his mind. Hutcheson never
returned to the council; the Carpenters returned a few
weeks later and Hutcheson's son Maurice took a council
seat at the bottom of the list. Meany was a prime mover
in 1952 in the endorsement of Adlai Stevenson for President
— only the second time in its history that the AFL had
endorsed a presidential candidate. He moved, too, against
the International Longshoremen's Association, which had
been found to be "corrupt" and gangster-dominated. When
the ILA refused to clean house, Meany had the union
expelled. He launched a rival union that tried unsuccess-
fully to win the bargaining rights held by the ILA. The
expulsion itself, though, forced the union to select new
leadership and to act more like a union. It returned to
the Federation several years later.

Meany's vigorous stand on gangsterism in the ILA
represented a sharp break with long-standing custom in
the AFL. The Federation had never directly intervened
in the affairs of an international union; the unions denied
it any such power. Meany's action, though, was a short,

but measurable, step toward a more centralized Federation.
It marked a definite narrowing of the freedom of action
when the two great union centers — the AFL and the CIO
of affiliated unions. The process was carried still further
— merged into a single federation.

Reuther and Meany moved toward the goal as the first
major business after becoming presidents of their respec-
tive federations. "The chief obstacle to unity," it was said,
was raiding — the practice of one union stealing another's
members. The first step toward unity was a historic no-
raiding agreement. It bound only those unions who signed
it, pledging them not to interfere in the established
bargaining relationships of another union. In six months,
65 of the AFL's 110 unions and 29 of the 32 CIO affiliates had signed, but these did not include the Carpenters,
the Teamsters, or the Steelworkers.

The joint unity committee moved to the question of
uniting the two bodies. "We can go after unity the long
way or the short way," Meany told the committee. "The
short way is to merge into one trade union center which
will protect the integrity of all affiliates. The long way is
to try to solve all our problems before merging. Which
will it be?" The committee chose "the short way." The
two centers would merge, making the affiliates of each
automatically affiliates of the new Federation. Each union
would keep its present jurisdiction; where there were two
unions with the same jurisdiction, the conflicting unions
would be encouraged to merge. Both craft and industrial
unions were recognized as necessary forms of organization.
The new body would be open to all workers regardless
of race, creed, color or national origin. It would be kept
free of corrupt influences and Communist infiltration. The
CIO would become the Industrial Union Department of

the new Federation, with equal status with the Building Trades, Metal Trades, and other departments. George Meany would be president, William F. Schnitzler secretary-treasurer. The new executive council would be made up of seventeen vice-presidents from the AFL, ten from the CIO. Its name would simply link their former names with "and." On December 5, 1955, in joint convention in New York City, with George Meany and Walter Reuther symbolically wielding a single gavel, unity was ratified.

It was at the start a restless and uncomfortable unity. Differences, both real and reported, between Meany and Reuther, between AFL and CIO unions and between their leaders, at times rocked the merger. But it held together.

It met a major challenge when a Senate committee under Senator John McClellan of Arkansas launched an investigation into "improper activities in labor-management relations." The McClellan probe quickly focused on corruption in unions, some of it real, some of it mere empty charges. Meany moved vigorously to meet the challenge implicit in the committee revelations of graft and corruption. At his insistence, the AFL-CIO adopted a series of "codes of ethics." He himself is said to have written the section on labor leaders who refuse, under the shelter of the Fifth Amendment, to testify on their conduct of their union's affairs. He insisted unions clean up their shady practices and get rid of officials involved in questionable practices. "I say we have no choice," Meany emphasized, "if a union allows its officers to conduct the union in a manner detrimental to the trade-union movement. We have no choice but to disassociate that union from the free association of unions that make up the AFL-CIO." Teamster President Dave Beck was ousted from the executive council. The Bakery and Confectionery Workers were

213

put under investigation (and later expelled). Other unions were ordered to clean up. Faced with sweeping charges of corruption in the Teamsters' Union, the AFL-CIO's largest affiliate, Meany moved no less vigorously.

When the question of expelling the Teamsters came before the convention, many voices were raised on their behalf. John F. English, the Teamsters' veteran secretary-treasurer, pleaded for a year's time to clean house. Woodruff Randolph, president of the Typographical Union, argued that the Federation had no authority to interfere in the internal affairs of an affiliate. "Autonomy," he declared, "is the rock on which the Federation had been founded." A good many delegates were keenly aware that, in their own bargaining and in strikes, the support of the Teamsters carried a high strategic value. James R. Hoffa, who had succeeded Beck as head of the Teamsters, wanted to stay in the Federation. He was reported to have offered a number of concessions — such as an outside caretaker for the union or supervision by a public "watchdog" committee. Meany turned down every offer. He reminded the delegates that when he took office as president of the AFL-CIO he had declared, "I will never surrender principle for expediency." He pointed out that the Teamsters had made no effort even to investigate their officers' "crimes against the labor movement." He put the question: "We have to free the membership from these men, from this dictatorship. The secretary will call the roll. You vote yes or no." The delegates voted yes. The Teamsters were expelled.

Meany's stubborn stand helped to make the Federation's codes of ethics effective standards of union conduct. It also increased, once again, the power of the Federation over the internal affairs of its affiliates. It did not emerge as anything like an all-powerful central government, but its influence was measurably greater. It was one more instance where the behavior of an individual union was made the business of the Federation. Such instances seem likely to increase, rather than decrease. Federal legislation — often at labor's insistence — reaches unendingly into new areas of national life. Federal decisions on the national budget, on taxes and interest rates are decisive in determining whether the nation prospers, whether unemployment rises or falls. Federal legislation sets the pattern for state and local programs, lays down the rules and pays the bills. The centralization of power in the labor movement, slow as it has been, moves with these developments in national life. It reflects labor's efforts to adjust to new times and new problems.

CHAPTER FOURTEEN

A. Philip Randolph

"Who appointed you as guardian
of the Negro members?"

A RESOLUTION at its 1959 convention demanded
that the AFL-CIO eliminate racially segregated
local unions, even though "some members" might
want to keep them. They are "morally wrong," the resolution said, "a violation . . . of free democratic trade
unionism." President Harry Bates of the Bricklayers objected. His union had a number of Negro locals, he said.
Many own their own halls, "are strong financially and the
membership does not want to be bothered. They want to
maintain those unions the same as they have over the
years. . . . We are going to keep those unions and maintain those conditions because if we don't we can't maintain
the conditions of the white unions." President Meany turned
to A. Philip Randolph, president of the Brotherhood of
Sleeping Car Porters and one of the resolution's authors.
"Will you consider it a violation . . . if the Bricklayers'
unions did not attempt to eliminate those segregated
unions . . . because the members do not want them
eliminated?" Randolph's reply was a simple, flat "yes."
Meany bluntly disagreed. "That is not my policy. I am

216

for the democratic rights of the Negro members. Who appointed you as a guardian of the Negro members in America?"

It was neither the first nor the last time that Randolph had been the center of heated argument on the floor of the AFL-CIO and AFL conventions, but it was probably one of the more notable ones. Appointed, elected and self-designated, Randolph had actually been a spokesman for the civil and economic rights of Negro workers for a good many years.

Asa Philip Randolph was born April 15, 1889, at Crescent City, Florida. His father was an itinerant Methodist preacher serving a circuit of several scattered and poor churches. The language of the Bible that he picked up from his father still echoes in Randolph's language. For years, the words, "Ye shall know the truth and the truth shall set you free," headed the brotherhood's publications. He and his brother went to public school, then to high school at Cookman Institute at Jacksonville, Florida. The two worked at every kind of odd job: running errands, selling papers, clerking in stores, shoveling dirt, loading flatcars, laying cross ties and rails.

Randolph went north after finishing high school. He attended night classes at the City College of New York, supporting himself by working as an elevator operator, porter, a waiter on the Fall River Line boats. He was fired as a waiter when he organized a protest against their living quarters on the boats. In 1917, with Chandler Owen, he started *The Messenger* — "The Only Radical Negro Magazine in America," the masthead said. He opposed World War I, protesting "the hypocrisy of the slogan, 'making the world safe for democracy,' when Negroes were lynched, jim-

217

Library of Congress

A. PHILIP RANDOLPH

A. *Philip Randolph*

crowed, disfranchised, and segregated in America." He was jailed briefly in Cleveland in 1918, and a paper referred to him as "the most dangerous Negro in America." He maintained his stand as a pacifist and a Socialist, ran for office several times on the Socialist ticket, lectured at the Rand School for Social Science in New York.

In the fall of 1925, Randolph was asked, as "an editor and labor advocate," to speak to a meeting of a Pullman Porters Athletic Association. Out of it came the Brotherhood of Sleeping Car Porters and an invitation to Randolph to become general organizer. He had never worked as a Pullman porter, knew little of their problems firsthand; but he accepted.

Many years before, when George Mortimer Pullman launched his sleeping car service, he had hired Negroes to act as porters. Negro labor was cheap; the Negro had a stereotyped reputation as "servile" and "impersonal." None of the railroad unions made places for them — even the American Railway Union, despite Gene Debs's efforts, refused them membership. The porters made several attempts to organize, but none succeeded. A Pullman Company official fired several of the ringleaders on one such occasion, commenting, "I thought it would be well to let them devote their entire time to it." Some came to know the feel of collective bargaining under the shelter of World War I labor policy. Soon after, though, the company established an employees' representation plan, and the porters' unions disappeared. Efforts to unionize in 1924 led the company to convene a wage conference under the employee representation plan. From it came a $7.50-a-month wage, plus tips; 11,000 miles was set as the porter's basic monthly service. The brotherhood claimed it took 350 to 400 hours

219

a month to fulfill a month's service. Tips — if times were good — averaged about $54 a month. Porters bought their own uniforms and incidentals — including the shoe polish they used while their patrons slept. They paid for their own meals, and overtime pay was less than they received for straight time. They were paid nothing for preparing cars and receiving passengers. Persistent demands of a crowded carful of patrons often prevented them from obtaining any reasonable rest.

Calling for "rights, not stripes" (a reference to the sleeve stripes the company awarded for length of service), Randolph set out on a tour of the country. Soon he had the help of porters who had been fired for union activities. One, Des Verney, gave up thirty-seven years of service toward his Pullman pension to go to work for the brotherhood. Few Negro leaders came to their aid; one who did was the poet James Weldon Johnson. He helped the porters obtain a $10,000 grant from the Garland Fund — money that helped to keep the brotherhood alive at a critical time.

The company utilized antiunion porters and inspectors to spy on the union men. It often invented excuses for discharging active members or for pulling them off the better-tipping runs. The brotherhood charged that agents of the Pullman Porters Benefit Association acted as "grafting and selfish Uncle Toms" and as "stool pigeons." The brotherhood met opposition from some Negro churches. Some who received contributions from antiunion sources provided forums for antiunion speakers. But one minister was offered $250 to refuse his church to brotherhood leaders; he turned it down. The Improved Benevolent Protective Order of Elks of the World denounced "all forms of unionism and economic radicalism as presented to us by white labor agitators and their tools." But two years later it endorsed the brotherhood. The Chicago *Defender*, a major Negro newspaper, at first opposed the union, later came to its support.

The brotherhood's initial efforts to gain recognition from the Pullman Company ended in failure. In March, 1928, the brotherhood's members approved a strike, 6,053 to 17. Randolph hoped the strike vote would bring government intervention under the Railway Labor Act. It set a deadline. The company hired new men, held them on call in Pullmans parked at the railroad stations. It posted extra porters at first stops — to take the place of crews who changed their minds after leaving the station. But the mediation board refused to act. The strike was postponed. Its inability to win recognition, soon assisted by the depression, resulted in an almost unending loss of members. Its income fell off. *The Messenger* was discontinued. In 1933, the brotherhood had only some seven hundred members.

But in 1934, with the help of the AFL, the brotherhood won an amendment to the Emergency Transportation Act. It gave the porters, finally, legal protection for their right to organize and bargain collectively. The brotherhood promptly challenged the Pullman Porters Protective Association for the right to represent them. They voted, 5,931 to 1,422, for the brotherhood. From the long, slow processes of negotiation and mediation, it emerged in 1937 with its first signed contract. It won the porters some two million dollars in pay increases, a reduction in monthly mileage from 11,000 to 7,000, a 240-hour month, and important improvements in their working conditions.

In 1928, the brotherhood had applied for a national union charter from the AFL. It was faced, then and later, with conflicting claims to its jurisdiction from other unions. It was not until 1936, after its victory in the mediation board election, that the brotherhood got its national charter. It was not, Randolph observed, "the result of a pious wish. The Pullman porters fought for it and won it."

Persistently, Randolph called on the Federation to aid the colored workers. He pushed through a resolution in 1934, despite the opposition of the resolutions committee, calling for an investigation of the conditions of colored workers. The report to the next year's convention concluded that only a few unions barred Negro workers — Meany said later twenty international unions had color bars in 1940. Where this happened, the report consoled, the Negro workers were accommodated by federal charters or segregated locals. Randolph asked the convention to enforce the traditional, nondiscriminatory position of the AFL. But President Green wanted to know: "Can we suspend the charter of an international union because it does not provide for the admission of colored members? . . . would you be willing to order that done?" The convention was not willing.

When World War II came, Randolph again protested against the contradiction he felt in the nation's war aims. He opposed fascism — and he later supported the war. "This war is different," he said. "In a Fascist state a minority group cannot struggle for equality." But he saw Negroes turned aside when they asked for work in national defense plants. Backed by the brotherhood, he called for a protest march on Washington. When President Roosevelt created the wartime Fair Employment Practices Commission, the march was "postponed." "Though I have found no Negroes who want to see the United Nations lose this war," Randolph said later, "I have found many who, before the war ends, want to see the stuffing knocked out of white supremacy and of empire over subject peoples." When Randolph attempted to win a postwar AFL endorsement of a permanent FEPC, the convention questioned whether such "compulsory control" was in keeping with the "freedom of association among the American people."

Some of the earliest Freedom Rides in North and South Carolina were planned in Randolph's office. A Pullman porter urged a boycott of city buses in Montgomery, Alabama; a young minister by the name of Martin Luther King was chosen to head it. In 1959, Randolph's resolution on eliminating segregated local unions precipitated the sharp exchange with President Meany. If the resolution were intended to put the AFL-CIO on record against segregated locals, President Meany finally said, "I think everybody here is in agreement with that." But it was understood that international unions would not proceed against segregated unions that refused to give up their charters.

With the prodding of Randolph and of the AFL-CIO, color bars disappeared from the union constitutions, and the list of Jim Crow locals shrunk. These, added to the pressures of the civil rights movement of recent years, have led the AFL-CIO to assume increasing responsibilities in the civil rights field — far beyond anything it or its predecessor had ever undertaken. The AFL-CIO has given strong support to civil rights legislation and to the group in Washington that is working for it. It has helped out, with money and manpower, in many civil rights efforts, often without asking or getting public credit. It has been a major supporter of a federal law requiring fair, nondiscriminatory hiring and˙on-the-job practices — an updated FEPC. It has insisted that unions be brought under such legislation. Civil rights has been given growing prominence in its goals — not in broad generalities but increasingly in terms of specific legislative proposals.

Progress has been slow. Soon after the debate at the 1959 convention, Randolph organized the Negro-American Labor Council to hurry it. He called on Negro members to rise in rebellion. "Organized labor will be shaken to its foundations," he said. "And we will not stop until we have cleansed labor's house of discrimination." Meany came to the NALC's third convention in 1962. "Frankly at the time," he told the group, "I did not think it was necessary. But I respect your motives and share your objectives." In 1963, the last Jim Crow clause in an international constitution was eliminated. In 1963, too, Meany invited Randolph to lead off the convention discussion of a far-reaching civil rights declaration. When Randolph organized a new march on Washington in 1963, the AFL-CIO sat passively by. Many unions were represented but not the Federation. In the 1965 Selma march, however, Meany saw to it that an AFL-CIO delegation took its place in line. In 1965, with Meany and Randolph leading the way, the convention adopted the "strongest" statement on civil rights in its history.

But unemployment among Negro workers persists at about twice the level of unemployment among whites. Randolph once pointed out that in 1837 Philadelphia Negroes made up 14 per cent of the poorhouse population, though they represented only 7 per cent of the general population. "This dusty statistic is an early example of a two-to-one relationship that has shown remarkable persistence down to the present." In many industries and skills, Negroes are underrepresented — the result of discrimination in hiring, apprenticeship and on-the-job treatment and of years of discrimination and segregation in education, housing and opportunity. The AFL-CIO supports fair-employment-practices laws and intensive union education to get at the former; it supports many types of training, antipoverty, housing, education and other programs to reach the latter. Its own staff departments work to encourage democratic practices on the job, in the unions and in the community. It is a major concern. "Even a little bit of discrimination is too much," President Meany once said. "It makes a mockery of our principles and it must be wiped out."

CHAPTER FIFTEEN

Postscript

T HE AFL-CIO observed its tenth birthday at its
San Francisco convention in 1965. The widely ex-
pressed fears — and some hope — that the merger
would not survive were almost completely erased. Many
of the earlier differences had been smoothed over or forgotten. The unanimity of the delegates on matters of policy
and program was so complete as to deprive the convention
of almost all debate or controversy. The Federation reported a gain in membership. It reported a long list of
legislative gains, along with a no less imposing list of
legislation it hoped to see passed. It could look back on
a still-growing effectiveness in raising the living standards
of American workers. Problems remained: the threat of
automation, knotty questions of civil rights, problems of
the working as well as the unemployed poor, the endlessly
complex task of adjusting its own practices and policies to
new times and new problems.

President Meany acknowledged his reelection with a
short speech of appreciation. The Federation had received
a report of "accomplishment in the legislative field. . . .

226

There is much to be done." Looking around, the trade union movement could see good contracts and good wages. "We see our unions making progress," he said, "but there are still too many people in America who are not sharing in the prosperity of this great nation."

In 1966, some eighteen million workers belonged to American trade unions. They represented one-quarter of the nation's total work force, but perhaps one-third of the nation's workers eligible for union membership. Some observers noted that the unions had reached a plateau and predicted they would climb no higher. And for some years membership had held remarkably steady. With the work force constantly growing, the trade unions came to represent a declining proportion of the nation's working people. More recent figures reflected an upturn in membership. How long it would continue or how high it would go, few dared say. But it was clear, even so, that the influence and the concerns of the trade union movement should, as they often did, reach far beyond its own members.

It came to this position — and to this realization — slowly and painfully. One of the major facts of union life has been, from the very start, the insistent, vigorous and often violent opposition of employers. The economic power of the employer — his final, absolute control of the job itself — has often been combined with the power of government and of the courts, of the press and the pulpit to the unions' disadvantage and defeat. Laws now seek to protect the workers' right to organize unions of their own choosing and to bargain collectively against the employers' power. The same laws have also transformed employer opposition. Antiunion laws and public relations activities are taking the place of labor spies and tear gas; psychological testing takes the place of the blacklist as a barrier to union-minded workers. Employer-controlled welfare plans bind him to his machine with golden threads. Opposition has simply shifted into more modern, more sophisticated channels.

In the face of unending opposition, the unionist has fought back with courage and persistence. He has been driven by a limitless hope for a decent — and constantly rising — standard of living, for shorter hours of work, for safer and cleaner workshops. Perhaps most of all, he has been driven by the powerful desire for recognition and personal dignity. He wanted, as Sylvis noted a hundred years ago, "independence and respectability . . . the means with which to educate our children and qualify them to play their part in the world's drama." His union became the tool for building better living standards and better jobs. He developed a system of law and procedures for protecting his job rights and insuring fair and impartial treatment. He built systems for providing broad health care and retirement programs.

More and more, though, he found himself going beyond his own job, his own union or industry. Trade unionists worked to outlaw tenement factories and sweatshops. They were a vital force in providing compensation for workers who were injured or killed on the job. They helped (if belatedly) to establish unemployment insurance. They were responsible for minimum wage laws and laws against child labor and laws establishing standards of safety and sanitation in the workshop. In these and countless other ways the unions helped millions of nonunion workers as well as their own members to enjoy a better break in our nation's industry.

But the interests of union members (even in these very broad terms) kept getting involved with still broader, still larger questions. Problems once might have been answered across the bargaining table or in the local community; now they could be answered only in the actions of a state legislature or of the federal government. Civil rights, housing, public education, basic questions of prosperity or depression became national questions. If labor was to protect its own interests, it, too, must become a force in national life. It used its influence to help win civil rights laws and advance equal opportunity. It joined in the war against poverty; it urged programs for more and better schools, homes, hospitals. Apart from the nation's older citizens themselves, trade unionists were the major supporters of Medicare. Increasingly, the social and economic and political planks in labor's platform spoke for millions of workers, not merely union members. Recognition spread slowly through the unions that they had to become the active and vocal conscience of the economy. Support for this idea varied widely — from one union to another, and at different times and different places. It was sometimes active and vigorous, at other times lazy and indifferent. Like every human institution, the trade union movement has its weaknesses, its foibles, just as it has its strengths and virtues. It has come a long way; it still has a long way to go. President Meany put it this way to the tenth convention of the AFL-CIO:

> We have to build a great deal more before we can take any satisfaction over our situation . . . we also must look forward with a sense of responsibility to the future. It has been said that the American trade union movement is the conscience of America . . . and this is true. The great mass of people who are still untouched by prosperity . . . you people sitting in this room are their representatives. Whether you will it or

229

not, you people sitting in this room are their representatives because they have no one else to represent them . . . the American trade union movement has a contribution to make.

However slowly or awkwardly or uncertainly the unions appear to build, this almost surely is their direction.

APPENDIX ONE

Glossary

Here is a short list of terms frequently used in trade union and industrial relations language. In compiling it, I have drawn heavily on (and I acknowledge with thanks) the far more comprehensive glossaries in *Speaking of Labor Unions* (International Labor Press Association, AFL-CIO, 1964), and *Glossary of Current Industrial Relations and Wage Terms* (Bulletin No. 1438, May, 1965, U. S. Department of Labor).

AFL-CIO: American Federation of Labor and Congress of Industrial Organizations. Federation of national and international unions formed in December, 1955, through merger of AFL and CIO.

American Federation of Labor (AFL): National federation of trade unions organized in 1886 as successor to Federation of Organized Trades and Labor Unions (1881). *See* Chapter 4.

apprentice: A person who enters into an agreement to learn a skilled trade or craft on the job under supervision

231

for a certain number of years and usually with related classroom work. Completion leads to status of
journeyman.

arbitration: Settlement of a labor dispute by the final and
binding decision of a third, neutral party (sometimes designated as impartial chairman or arbitra-
tor). In the nineteenth century, the term was sometimes used loosely to refer to peaceful settlement
of disputes through negotiation or mediation.

back-to-work movement: Return to work of some or all
striking workers without achieving purposes of strike,
often promoted and organized by management.

bargaining unit: A group of employees that a union may
appropriately represent in collective bargaining.
Now, usually determined by National Labor Relations Board.

blacklist: A list of employees deemed "undesirable" as
employees and denied employment, formerly applied frequently to union organizers and active
union leaders.

boycott: A campaign, often by a union or group of unions,
to discourage the purchase, handling or use of
products or services of a nonunion producer or of an
employer involved in a labor dispute.

business agent: A full-time, paid representative of a union,
either elected or appointed, to enforce terms of
union contract, adjust grievances with the employer,
handle the union's business. Sometimes an organizer,
too. A "walking delegate."

central labor body: A group of unions in a specified geographical area such as a city or county or state.
Earlier, they were referred to as a "trades union"

232

and sometimes as a local "federation" or central labor union.

checkoff: The employer by mutual agreement withholds dues and assessments from employees' paychecks and pays them directly to the employees' union.

closed shop: The employer agrees to hire and retain only members of the union. Important difference from union shop is that in a closed shop employer will hire only union members. Now prohibited by law.

collective bargaining: The process of determining the conditions of employment (wages, hours, work rules, etc.) by negotiations between an employer or group of employers and the representative, usually a union, of the employees.

company union: A union made up of employees of a single employer, often organized or inspired by the employer and dominated by him. In this sense, it is now outlawed.

Congress of Industrial Organizations (CIO): Federation of national and international unions formed in 1938 from the Committee for Industrial Organization. The latter group had its origin in a group of AFL unions in 1935. *See* Chapter 8.

craft union: A trade union that basically limits its membership to workers trained in a particular craft or skill or working in a closely related trade. Sometimes called a "horizontal" union, since its members usually work in a variety of industries. Examples: carpenters, printers, bricklayers. Many former craft unions now include industrial members. SEE *industrial union*.

dual union: Term applied by one union to a rival union

seeking to represent workers in the same craft or industry.

fair employment practices: Such practices forbid discrimination in hiring, promotion, discharge or in the conditions of employment on grounds of race, creed, color or national origin and, in some cases, sex and age. Now enforced by federal law through Fair Employment Practices Commissions (FEPC) and U. S. Equal Employment Opportunity Commission (1965).

grievance: Complaint or dissatisfaction of employee with conditions of employment or treatment on job or charging violation of union contract.

hiring hall: A place where out-of-work members (and, now, nonmembers) may apply or be referred or dispatched for work. Operated by unions or jointly by unions and employers.

hot cargo: Goods made or shipped by nonunion labor or strikebreakers, which union members sometimes refuse to handle.

industrial union: A union that takes in all or most of the workers in a single industry. Sometimes called "vertical" union, because it takes in all grades of skill, from lowest to highest in particular industry. Examples: auto workers, steelworkers.

injunction: Court order prohibiting employer or union (and often its officers and members) from performing some act that court believes would result in irreparable injury or damage to property or other rights.

international union: A union with members in Canada as well as the United States. Often used interchangeably with *national union*.

ironclad: SEE *yellow dog contract.*

journeyman: A fully qualified craftsman, usually as result of completing apprenticeship.

jurisdiction: The particular skill or craft, industry, or geographical area in which a union claims the right to represent the workers. A conflict between unions over which shall represent certain workers or whose members shall do a certain kind of work is a *jurisdictional dispute.*

lockout: A labor dispute in which the employer (or group of employers) withholds or denies further employment to his employees. An employer weapon to compel employees to accept his terms.

mediation: Attempt by a third party to assist or encourage the settlement of a labor dispute by suggesting terms or methods of settlement but without any power to compel either union or employer to accept.

National Labor Relations Board (NLRB): Board created under Wagner Act and continued under the National Labor-Management Relations Act to supervise representation elections and decide cases arising from unfair labor practices committed by employers or unions.

open shop: An unorganized establishment or shop where union membership is not required. (SEE *union shop.*) Also, establishment with policy of refusing to recognize or deal with union and, in effect, closed to union members.

picket: A person posted at or near employer's place of business to advertise existence of labor dispute or nonunion conditions, intended to discourage others from taking the places of the strikers or from patronizing the employer.

rank and file: Members of an organization other than its officers and employees.

scab: A worker in a struck plant; a worker who continues on the job during a strike; strikebreaker.

seniority: The worker's length of service, often used to determine order in which employees are laid off, promoted, given choice of vacations, etc.

speedup: Management-forced increase in speed of work without corresponding increase in pay. May require tending more machines or covering more territory (stretchout) or working faster to keep up with assembly line.

strike: Concerted stoppage of work by employees (not necessarily members of a union) to express a grievance or achieve some change or improvement in conditions of their jobs. *Slowdown strike*: Deliberate reduction in output or speed of work. *Sitdown strike*: Employees report for work but remain idle inside workshop; now illegal. *Sympathy strike*: Strike by workers not directly involved in dispute to express support of other strikers. *General strike*: A rare stoppage of work by all workers in a country or other geographical area; in garment trades, a strike of all crafts against all employers in a particular section of industry or a particular area.

trade union: Originally a craft union but now used for any union.

union: A voluntary organization of workers to deal as a group (collectively) with their employer in setting the conditions and resolving other problems relating to their employment and to act as a group in political, community and other areas of common interest.

236

union recognition: Employer acceptance of the union as the bargaining representative of his employees.

union shop: A contract clause requiring employees to become members of a union usually thirty to ninety days after being hired and to remain members in good standing as a condition of employment.

yellow dog contract: An agreement demanded by an employer in which the employee agrees, as a condition of being hired and keeping the job, not to join — or remain a member of — a union.

APPENDIX TWO

Biographical Data

WILLIAM H. SYLVIS. Born November 26, 1828, Armagh, Pennsylvania. A molder by trade, he became a determined and dedicated unionist. Helped found Molders' International Union (1859) and served as its president (1863-69). A leader in organizing the short-lived National Labor Union; death (1869) cut short his first term as its president.

TERENCE V. POWDERLY. Born January 22, 1849, Carbondale, Pennsylvania. A machinist by trade, an early member of the Machinists' and Blacksmiths' Union. Succeeded founder Uriah Stephens as Grand Master Workman of the Knights of Labor (1879), held office until 1893. President McKinley appointed him to Immigration Bureau; President Theodore Roosevelt fired him but subsequently reinstated him. Died 1924.

SAMUEL GOMPERS. Born in London, England, January 27, 1850, came to United States in 1863. Active member of Cigarmakers' International Union and president of Local 144 (1875). Helped organize the feeble Federation of Organized Trades and Labor Unions (1881). Elected first president of the newly formed American Federation of Labor (1886), a post he held with the exception of one year (1894-95) until death in 1924. An important figure in mobilization of industry and manpower in World War I, presided over the postwar international commission that created the International Labor Organization.

EUGENE V. DEBS. Born November 5, 1855, Terre Haute, Indiana. At fourteen went to work on Vandalia Railroad. First secretary of Vigo Lodge, No. 16, of the Brotherhood of Locomotive Firemen (1875). Served as assistant editor of brotherhood's *Magazine,* then as grand secretary and editor (1880-92). Organized American Railway Union (1893), which was routed and destroyed a year later in the great railway strike and Pullman boycott. Ran five times as Socialist Party candidate for President, his last campaign being conducted from jail cell at Atlanta, Georgia, where he was imprisoned as a result of his outspoken opposition to World War I. Died 1926.

WILLIAM D. "BIG BILL" HAYWOOD. Born February 4, 1869, Salt Lake City, Utah. Educated in schools and streets of Salt Lake City and several mining camps. Became a "hard rock" miner, joined Western Federation of Miners (1896), elected to its executive board, then secretary-treasurer (1900). Helped found Industrial Workers of the World (1905). Jailed – and eventually acquitted – of charges that he conspired to murder Frank Steunenberg, former governor of Idaho. Fired from WFM, he became a militant leader, then general secretary, of the IWW. Arrested and jailed with hun-

239

dreds of other Wobblies in 1918. While out on bail, facing heavy fines and prison term, he fled to the Soviet Union, where he died in 1928.

WILLIAM GREEN. Born March 3, 1873, Coshocton, Ohio. Went to work with his father in coal mines. Climbed the ladder of union offices, became chief statistician of United Mine Workers, elected to two terms in Ohio State Senate (1911-15); chosen secretary-treasurer of UMW and seventh vice-president of AFL (1913). Elected as compromise successor to Sam Gompers as president of AFL (1924), he headed Federation through the years of the Great Depression, the AFL-CIO conflict, the AFL's sharp resurgence. Died 1952.

JOHN L. LEWIS. Born February 12, 1880, Lucas, Iowa. The son of a miner, a miner himself, he became president of miners' local union at Panama, Illinois (1909); legislative representative of UMW Illinois district (1911); served as AFL special representative, UMW statistician, vice-president, finally (1921) elected president. He led industrial-union forces that formed Committee for Industrial Organization (1935), became first president of Congress of Industrial Organizations (1938). Resigned that post after bitterly opposing reelection of Franklin Delano Roosevelt in 1940. Led Mine Workers in several angry and unpopular wartime and postwar strikes. Retired from UMW presidency in 1960.

SIDNEY HILLMAN. Born March 23, 1887, in Lithuania. Arrested twice for underground political activities. Emigrated to Chicago in 1907. Learned garment cutter's trade, won recognition in dramatic strike of clothing workers at Hart, Schaffner and Marx, greater recognition yet for his part in developing unique system of

240

industrial relations that grew from the strike. When several groups of garment workers seceded from AFL United Garment Workers and formed Amalgamated Clothing Workers of America, Hillman was chosen as president. A major figure in the National Recovery Administration (1933) and in the national defense program (1940). Organized CIO Political Action Committee (1943) and helped to form World Federation of Trade Unions (1945). Died 1946.

DAVID DUBINSKY. Born February 22, 1893, Brest-Litovsk; learned the baker's craft in his father's bakery in Lodz, Russian Poland. He quickly became involved in underground union activities, was arrested twice and exiled to Siberian village. He escaped, made his way home, then emigrated to New York. Learned the garment cutter's trade, joined Local 10 of the International Ladies Garment Workers Union. Became general manager of Local 10 (1921); secretary-treasurer of ILGWU (1929), president (1932). Active supporter of CIO until permanent organization formed in 1938. Returned to AFL in 1940. Led ILGWU in developing wide-ranging welfare, educational, political activities. Active figure in defeating World Federation of Trade Unions and in forming International Confederation of Free Trade Unions. Retired from ILGWU presidency in 1966.

PHILIP MURRAY. Born May 25, 1886, in Glasgow, Scotland, the son of a miner. Came to United States with his father in 1902, went to work in mines around Pittsburgh. He was fired for slugging checkweighman; miners made him president of local union. Elected to UMW executive board (1912), president of UMW District 5 (1916), vice-president of UMW (1921). Headed

CIO Steel Workers' Organizing Committee (1936), led steelworkers in forming United Steelworkers of America (1942). Succeeded John L. Lewis as president of CIO (1940). Died December, 1952.

WALTER REUTHER. Born September 1, 1907, Wheeling, West Virginia, son of brewery worker and vigorous unionist. Became toolmakers' apprentice when sixteen. Fired from Wheeling Steel for attempting to organize union, he went to Detroit and took jobs in auto plants, first at Briggs, then Ford. Laid off, he and brother Victor took prolonged world tour, returned to join in organizing union of auto workers. Won presidency of United Auto Workers (1946), succeeded Philip Murray as president of CIO (1952). Collaborated in uniting AFL and CIO (1955).

GEORGE MEANY. Born August 16, 1894, New York City. Son of a plumber who headed his local union, he started apprenticeship when sixteen. Became business agent of Local 463 (1922), secretary of New York Building Trades Council (1923). Elected president, New York State Federation of Labor (1934). Succeeded Frank Morrison as secretary-treasurer of AFL (1939), William Green as president (1952). Architect of AFL-CIO unity, Meany was chosen first president of combined organization (1955).

A. PHILIP RANDOLPH. Born April 15, 1889, Crescent City, Florida. Son of itinerant minister, he worked at numerous odd jobs while finishing education. As "editor and labor advocate," asked to help organize Brotherhood of Sleeping Car Porters. Led long, ultimately successful fight for recognition of brotherhood. Major figure in obtaining fair employment practices by presidential order (1941) as aftermath of proposed march on Washington. Leader of 1963 march on Washington. Founded Negro-American Labor Council (1960) to oppose racial discrimination in labor movement.

APPENDIX THREE

Some notes on further reading

THE PLACE to start is with the long-focus, wide-angle view — the general histories of labor. One of the most readable is Thomas R. Brooks, *Toil and Trouble* (Dell Publishing Co., New York, 1964). Commons and Associates, *History of Labour in the United States* (The Macmillan Co., New York, 1918-) put down a classic pattern of solid, largely unadorned fact; the first two volumes are especially valuable. Selig Perlman, *A History of Trade Unionism in the United States* (The Macmillan Co., New York, 1922) sums it up in relatively small space. Philip Taft, *Organized Labor in American History* (Harper & Row, New York, 1964) supplies much more detail. Philip S. Foner, *History of the Labor Movement in the United States* (International Publishers, New York, 1947-), as far as it has gone in four volumes, offers an even wider-ranging abundance of detail, presented from a radical, Marxist point of view. Louis Adamic, *Dynamite* (Peter Smith, Gloucester, Mass., 1963) combines a radical viewpoint and a strong sense of outrage in a dramatic telling of labor's story. Samuel

244

Yellen, *American Labor Struggles* (Harcourt, Brace, New York, 1936) recounts the drama of selected episodes.

Two volumes of biographical sketches introduce some of labor's champions. They are Bruce Minton and John Stuart, *Men Who Lead Labor* (Modern Age Books, New York, 1937) and Charles Madison, *American Labor Leaders* (Frederick Ungar Publishing Co., New York, 1962). Elias Lieberman, *Unions Before the Bar* (Harper & Bros., New York, 1950) focuses on labor's fate in the courts.

Other volumes supply greater detail about the men themselves. James C. Sylvis, *The Life, Speeches, Labors and Essays of William H. Sylvis,* found little fault with his more famous brother. Charlotte Todes, *William H. Sylvis and the National Labor Union* (International Publishers, New York, 1942) sums up Sylvis' story from a left-wing viewpoint in far less space.

T. V. Powderly is his own most amusing biographer — and probably his friendliest, too — in *Thirty Years of Labor* (Excelsior Publishing House, Columbus, Ohio, 1889) and *The Path I Trod* (Columbia University Press, New York, 1940). Norman J. Ware, *The Labor Movement in the United States, 1860-1895* (Vintage Books, New York, 1964) offers a more critical view of Powderly and the Knights of Labor. Sam Gompers tells his own story at great length in *Seventy Years of Life and Labor* (New York, 1925). He figures prominently, of course, in almost every general history of American labor. I have written his story for young people in *Sam Gompers: Labor's Pioneer* (Abelard-Schuman, New York, 1964).

Eugene V. Debs's story is recorded with warmth in McAlister Coleman, *Eugene V. Debs: A Man Unafraid* (Greenberg, New York, 1930); with affection in David

Karsner, *Debs: His Authorized Life and Letters* (Boni and Liveright, New York, 1919); in overgenerous detail in Ray Ginger, *The Bending Cross* (Rutgers University Press, New Brunswick, N. J., 1949). Still another view is in my own work, mainly for young people, *Eugene V. Debs: Rebel, Labor Leader, Prophet* (Lothrop, Lee & Shepard Co., New York, 1966). Big Bill Haywood tells his own story, but none too well, in *Bill Haywood's Book* (International Publishers, New York, 1929). The I.W.W. is reflected drily in Paul F. Brissenden, *The I.W.W.: A Study of American Syndicalism* (Russell & Russell, New York, 1957); happily if somewhat romantically, in Joyce L. Kornbluh, *Rebel Voices* (University of Michigan Press, Ann Arbor, 1964).

William Green's story is told in Max Danish, *William Green,* and is frequently encountered in many more general works. John L. Lewis has been covered by countless reporters, with more surely to come. Cecil Carnes, the author of *John L. Lewis: Leader of Labor* (Robert Speller Publishing Corp., New York, 1936) is an early admirer; Saul Alinsky is even more fawning in his so-called "unauthorized biography": *John L. Lewis* (G. P. Putnam's Sons, New York, 1949). James A. Wechsler, *Labor Baron* (William Morrow and Co., New York, 1944) takes an opposite view. Perhaps the best of them is McAlister Coleman, *Men and Coal* (Farrar & Rinehart, Inc., Toronto, 1943).

Jean Gould, *Sidney Hillman: Great American* (Houghton Mifflin Co., Boston, 1952) is written especially for young people. Matthew Josephson, *Sidney Hillman: Statesman of American Labor* (Doubleday & Co., New York, 1952) encompasses far greater scope and detail. Benjamin Stolberg, *Tailor's Progress* (Doubleday, Doran & Co., New York, 1944) records the progress of David Dubinsky, as does

246

Max Danish, *The World of David Dubinsky* (World Publishing Co., Cleveland and New York, 1957). Philip Murray's role is pieced together mostly from a variety of contemporary sources, as is the still unfinished story of George Meany. Irving Howe and B. J. Widick, *The UAW and Walter Reuther* (Random House, New York, 1949) takes on the whole a favorable view of Walter Reuther; Eldorous L. Dayton, *Walter Reuther: Aristocrat of the Bargaining Table* (The Devin-Adair Co., New York, 1958) offers a sharply different, right-wing view. Much too little has been written about Philip Randolph. The story of his union's struggles is told, academically, in Brailsford R. Brazeal, *The Brotherhood of Sleeping Car Porters* (Harper & Bros., New York, 1946); he appears all too briefly in Edwin R. Embree, *13 Against the Odds* (The Viking Press, New York, 1944). ·

Still other volumes throw a sharp light on particular periods. For the period of the Twenties, turn to Irving Bernstein, *The Lean Years* (Houghton Mifflin Co., Boston, 1960). Also of interest is Arthur M. Schlesinger, Jr., *The Age of Roosevelt,* especially the first two volumes, *The Crisis of the Old Order* and *The Coming of the New Deal* (Houghton Mifflin Co., Boston, 1957 and 1959). Walter Galenson, *The CIO Challenge to the AFL* (Harvard University Press, 1960) details the rise of the CIO in the latter Thirties.

And so on. These references are, by no means, the whole of it; they barely touch the surface. But they run a gamut of viewpoint and style and substance. They are a beginning.

DAVID F. SELVIN

Index

249

Master Workman, 38; eight-hour day, 43; Gompers, 45, 46; ousted as Grand Master Workman, 47; death, 47, 238
printers, New York, 16
Progressive Cigarmakers, 45
Progressive Miners of America, 124
Progressive Party, 185
Protocol of Peace, 162, 163, 171
Pullman Company, 220, 221
Pullman, George Mortimer, 81, 88
Pullman Porters Athletic Association, 219
Pullman Porters Benefit Association, 220
Pullman strike, boycott, 82-89

railroads, 17
Randolph, A. Philip, 216-225: early years, 217; heads Brotherhood of Sleeping Car Porters, 219; wins AFL charter, 222; civil rights, 222. *See also* 242
Randolph, Woodruff, 214
Raskin, A. H., 202
Reed, John, 104
Republic Steel, 135, 181
Richert, Thomas, 142, 147
Reuther, Jacob, 188
Reuther, Valentine, 188
Reuther, Victor, 189
Reuther, Walter, 188-202: early years, 189; world tour, 189; helps organize auto workers, 193; Reuther "plans", 197; president of United Auto Workers, 200. *See also* 186, 212-213, 242
Romney, George, 197

Roosevelt, President Franklin D., 114, 137, 138, 153, 154, 169, 184, 207, 222
Roosevelt, President Theodore, 64, 69, 99
Rosenwald, Julius, 167

Schaffner, Joseph, 142
Schlesinger, Arthur, Jr., 116, 119
Schlessinger, Benjamin, 166, 168
Schnitzler, William F., 211
Sears Roebuck Company, 146
Selma march, 224
Sherman Anti-Trust Act, 63
Sigman, Morris, 166
Siney, John, 33
Sinexon, Henry L., 35
Social Democracy of America, 89
Socialists, 58-60, 88-90, 91, 188
Stanton, Elizabeth Cady, 30
Steel Workers Organizing Committee, 130, 133-135. *See also* 175-187
Stephens, Uriah S., 35, 38, 45
Steunenberg, Frank, 90, 96, 99
Stevenson, Adlai, 211
Stolberg, Benjamin, 165
Strasser, Adolph, 45, 51
strikes: Philadelphia carpenters, *1791*, 16; Chicago, Burlington and Quincy, 77; cigarmakers, 51; cloakmakers, 160; Coeur d'Alene, 92, 96; Colorado, 97; eight-hour day, *1886*, 53; General Motors, 131, 199; Gould's southwestern lines, *1886*, 46; Great Northern, 79; Hart Schaffner and Marx, 141; Homestead, 57, 175; Kelsey-Hayes Wheel Corp., 193; Lawrence textile workers,